Healthy Me

Healthy Me

Fun Ways to Develop
Good Health and Safety Habits

Activities for Children 5 to 8

MICHELLE O'BRIEN-PALMER

CHICAGO
REVIEW
PRESS

Library of Congress Cataloging-in-Publication Data

O'Brien-Palmer, Michelle.
   Healthy me : fun ways to develop good health and safety habits :   activities for children 5–8 / Michelle O'Brien-Palmer.
      p.   cm.
   Includes bibliographical references.
   Summary: Teaches health and safety through over seventy creative projects, recipes, and experiments.
   ISBN 1-55652-359-9
      1. Children—Health and hygiene—Experiments Juvenile literature.
   2. Accidents—Prevention—Experiments Juvenile literature.
   [1.Health—Experiments.   2. Safety—Experiments.   3. Experiments.   4. Handicraft.]   I. Title
   RA777.024 1999
   613'.0432—dc21   99-20860
                                                                                            CIP

Design and illustrations: © 1999 by Fran Lee

© 1999 by Michelle O'Brien-Palmer
All rights reserved
Published by Chicago Review Press, Incorporated
814 North Franklin Street
Chicago, Illinois 60610
ISBN 1-55652-359-9
Printed in the United States of America

5 4 3 2 1

Healthy Me is respectfully dedicated to my mentors,
the late **Dr. Dorothy Nyswander** and the late **Sarah Mazelis**.
Their significant contributions to the field of health education
have provided the foundation for my work.

Contents

Healthy Me

In order to stay healthy, there are things I need to do.
I keep myself clean and I brush my chompers, too.
I eat good food and exercise each day
So I'll grow big and strong and have energy to play.

Sung to "The Itsy Bitsy Spider"

Introduction for Parents and Teachers

Healthy Me is about learning how to stay healthy and safe. It invites children to embrace health-promoting habits through fun, relevant, and purposeful activities. The first chapter, "Clean Machine," explores all aspects of staying clean, from microbes to soap making. "Healthy Chompers," the second chapter, delves into fun tooth facts and projects from plaque testing to weaving a floss key chain. Healthy alternatives to processed snack foods in wonderful recipes designed to delight are featured in the third chapter, "Nutritious and Delicious." In the fourth chapter, "Exercising My Muscles," exciting exercise activities elevate the child's understanding of water intake requirements, the importance of stretching before exercise, and fun exercise options in Bingo Boards. The fifth chapter, "Safe and Sound," takes children through a number of engaging safety activities designed to reinforce positive habits, like wearing seat belts and helmets, as well as teaching how to dial 9-1-1 and cross the street safely.

Each activity is designed to be fun and simple and to promote learning by engaging children in a process of self-discovery. Even young children become scientists as they predict outcomes, gather materials, make scientific observations, and respond to their findings. These hands-on activities provide instant information and introduce children to the scientific process of discovery that they will use in their scientific inquiries for the rest of their lives.

The structure of each *Healthy Me* activity reflects the progression used in any scientific exploration. The basic concepts have been preserved as children are transitioned into the process of discovery using language that is familiar to them. Each activity begins with the phrase "Did you know?" which corresponds to research and new information. "You will need" introduces children to the materials needed to conduct their experiments. With the phrase "What do you think?" every activity allows the child to make an outcome prediction, or hypothesis. "Now you are ready to" explains the procedure one would follow in testing the hypothesis. The "Brain exercise" gives children an opportunity to draw conclusions from their scientific observations.

Each chapter begins with a poem that can be sung to a familiar tune. The chapter contents are described in

"In . . . you will find." Journal sheets are provided in each chapter to help children record and reflect as they connect language, artwork, and learning. Make as many copies as you need.

The last chapter references lively, fact-filled nonfiction books that will help you delve even further into the topics covered through the activities. This chapter also features a list of recommended products, along with the manufacturer's address and current (as of printing) prices.

All activities have been field-tested successfully in homes and classrooms. Most require simple materials that can be easily adjusted to accommodate your children. In these cases exact quantities of materials have not been specified. Estimated yields are given when appropriate for food recipes.

Initially, all of the activities will require adult supervision. After completing the activities together, many teachers and parents choose to set up learning centers using some of the activity materials on the topic being explored. This is a great way to extend and expand learning.

Healthy Me is an exploration of self. As children explore staying healthy, they will develop excellent lifelong health habits. They'll learn how to stay safe and practice safety techniques. Join your children as they delve into wonderful ways to stay healthy and safe.

Clean Machine

I Wash My Hands

I wash my hands before I eat
Fruit so sweet or veggie treats.
I wash my hands before I eat,
Before I take my seat.

Soap and water work just right.
Germs they fight with all their might.
Soap and water work just right
To clean me day and night.

Sung to "Mary Had a Little Lamb"

4

In Clean Machine you will find

My Clean Machine Journal

Today I learned

Keeping Clean—Staying Healthy

What should I know about keeping clean?

✪ It is important to keep your hands, your hair, and the rest of your body clean so that you will stay healthy.

✪ Microbes can be mold spores (seeds that will grow to be mold), bacteria, or viruses. They are too small for you to be able to see them. Sometimes bacteria and viruses are called *germs*.

✪ Germs like to live in warm, moist places, like your hands. Since your hands touch many things, lots of germs end up on them. Germs can make you sick.

✪ One easy way to get rid of germs is to wash your hands with soap and warm water. Soap holds onto the germs and dirt on your skin and then carries them down the drain with the water.

✪ You can't see germs, but every time you sneeze or cough, you blow out millions of them. This is why it is so important to catch those germs in a tissue. Remember to cover your mouth and nose when you sneeze and cover your mouth when you cough! Your friends will be glad you did.

1 Grow and Show—A Handful of Microbes

Did you know?

Microbes can be mold spores, bacteria, or viruses. Your hands collect microbes as they go through the day. The virus and bacteria microbes are sometimes called germs. They can make you sick.

You will need

1 can (10½ ounces) tomato soup

Can opener (use with adult supervision)

Measuring cup

1 jar lid (plastic peanut butter jar lids work very well)

Plastic storage container

Refrigerator

Permanent marker

1 resealable plastic sandwich bag

1 cotton swab, like a Q-tip

Your hand

Rack to elevate the growing lid

Room-temperature environment

Magnifying glass

Colored pencils

See and Draw Observation Diary I, page 11, copied onto white paper

What do you think?

If my partner touches my hand with the cotton swab and then gently rubs the swab over the tomato soup in the lid, microbes (will) or (won't) grow on the soup.

Now you are ready to

1. Carefully open the tomato soup can with the can opener. Pour approximately ¼ cup of uncooked, undiluted tomato soup into the jar lid. Pour the remaining soup into a plastic container with a lid and store it in the refrigerator.
2. Use the permanent marker to write your name and the date in the top left corner of the sandwich bag.
3. Take a cotton swab and rub it over the inside of your hand in a Z pattern.
4. Gently rub the swab over the surface of the tomato soup in a Z pattern. Carefully place the lid in the labeled sandwich bag and seal. Throw the swab away.

5. Place the lid up on a rack, like a cookie-cooling rack, on a table where it can be easily viewed.
6. View the lid every day for a week. Use your colored pencils to record your daily observations in your See and Draw Observation Diary I, page 11.
7. After observing the sealed lid for a week, throw it away.

Brain exercise

When the microbes grew on the tomato mixture, they were . . .

Activity Goal	Health Note	Key to Success	Hint
To grow microbe colonies from the germs and spores on our hands.	Microbes are in the air and all around us. They are too small for us to see. Once they get the nutrients they need to grow, they will multiply and we will be able to see the microbe colonies.	This activity needs to be carefully monitored. The lid needs to be kept inside the sealed sandwich bag so that the children don't breathe in potentially harmful microbes. Remember to throw the sealed lid away on the seventh day.	The growth doesn't usually show until after the second or third observation day. Small clear plastic flower-pot water trays work very well as lids. If you are working with a large group of children, use one lid per child with separate cotton swabs. Refrigerate leftover tomato soup for use in activity #3, They're Everywhere! Microbe Check, on page 13.

② See and Draw Observation Diaries

Did you know?
Scientists record their scientific findings in pictures and words.

You will need
Colored pencils
See and Draw Observation Diary I, page 11
See and Draw Observation Diary II, page 12

Now you are ready to
1. Observe the tomato soup in the lid(s).
2. Is anything growing on the soup?
3. What colors do you see?
4. Use your colored pencils to draw what you see inside the circle(s) in the observation diary.
5. Write the information asked for in the diary.

Activity Goal	Health Note	Key to Success	Hint
To record scientific observations in an observation diary.	It is very important that the bags holding the soup samples be kept sealed.	This activity needs to be carefully monitored. It is easier and more fun when the adult keeps a diary, too.	If the plastic bag is fogged up over the organisms, slide the lid into a better viewing position inside the bag.

See and Draw Observation Diary I

Microbes from My Hand

Observations made by _____
                                              (your name)

Observations made on _____
                                              (today's date)

See and Draw Observation Diary II

Microbes from Different Objects

Swab #1 _____

Swab #2 _____

Swab #3 _____

Swab #4 _____

Observations made by _____ **On** _____
(your name)   (today's date)

③ They're Everywhere! Microbe Check

Did you know?
Microbes can live on tables, floors, books, and other objects.

You will need
1 can (10½ ounces) tomato soup

Can opener (use with adult supervision)

Measuring cup

4 large jar lids (plastic peanut butter jar lids work very well)

4 cotton swabs, like Q-tips

Permanent marker

4 resealable plastic sandwich bags

Table

Floor

Doorknob

Book

Rack to elevate the growing lids

Room-temperature environment

Magnifying glass

See and Draw Observation Diary II, page 12, copied 7 times onto white paper

What do you think?
If I touch objects with a cotton swab and then gently rub the swab over the surface of the tomato soup, microbes (will) or (won't) grow on the soup.

Now you are ready to
1. Open the tomato soup can with the can opener. Pour approximately ¼ cup of uncooked, undiluted tomato soup into each of the jar lids, or use the soup left over from activity #1.
2. Take a cotton swab and rub it over the top of a table in a Z pattern.
3. Use the permanent marker to write the name of the object tested and the date on the top left corner of the sandwich bag.
4. Gently rub the swab in a Z pattern across the surface of the tomato soup in one of the lids. Carefully place the lid in the labeled sandwich bag and seal.
5. Place the lid up on a rack on a table where it can be easily viewed.
6. Repeat steps 2 through 5 using the floor, a door knob, and a book.

7. View the lids every day for a week. Draw pictures of what you see in your See and Draw Observation Diary II, page 12.

8. On the seventh day, throw the lids away.

Brain exercise
When the microbes grew on the tomato soup mixture lids, they were . . .

book

door

floor

Activity Goal

To grow microbes from ordinary objects.

Health Note

The most visible growth will be from mold spores. However, other microbes reside on these items as well. Hand washing helps to remove the microbes we pick up when touching objects and other people.

Key to Success

This activity needs to be carefully monitored. The lids need to be kept safely inside the sealed sandwich bags so that the children don't breathe in any potentially harmful microbes. The sealed bags need to be thrown away on the seventh observation day.

Hint

One can of tomato soup makes exactly four growing dishes. The growth in the lids isn't usually visible until after the second or third day. Ask children to name other objects in your home or classroom that they would like to test.

④ Pretty Sticky—Oil and Dirt

Did you know?
Microbes and dirt stick to oil.

You will need
Table or work space covered with newspaper
2 paper plates
1 spoon
2 spoonfuls dirt
1 large drop cooking oil

What do you think?
If I pour dirt on a paper plate covered with oil, the dirt (will) or (won't) stick to the oil.

Now you are ready to
1. Place the 2 paper plates in separate locations on the table.
2. Pour 1 spoonful of dirt on the first paper plate.
3. Turn the plate over facedown, using the newspaper to catch any debris. Flip it right side up and observe the plate.
4. Pour a large drop of cooking oil onto the second paper plate. Tilt the plate back and forth to spread the oil evenly.
5. Spread 1 spoonful of dirt over the oily section of the paper plate.
6. Turn the plate containing the oil and dirt facedown. Observe the plate. What happened to the dirt? Why do you think this happened?

Brain exercise
Oil makes the dirt . . .

Activity Goal	Health Note	Key to Success	Hint
To show children how dirt sticks to oil.	Dirt and microbes stick to the natural oil found on our hands.	Do this activity prior to activity #5, Oily Me? Fingerprints Will Tell, on page 16.	This activity can be messy, but it is worth the trouble.

5   Oily Me? Fingerprints Will Tell

Did you know?
Your skin has natural oils to keep it soft.

You will need
New colored plastic cup
Baby powder

What do you think?
If I touch a plastic cup, I (will) or
(won't) leave fingerprints on it.

Now you are ready to
1. Hold the cup in your hand as if you were going to drink out of it.
2. Put the cup down and sprinkle a little baby powder around the outside of the cup.
3. Gently tap the cup to remove the excess powder. What happened? Can you see your fingerprints?
4. Ask a friend to touch the cup. Use the baby powder to see if his/her fingerprints show.

Brain exercise
When I touched the cup, the oil on my fingers . . .

Activity Goal	Health Note	Key to Success	Hint
To see the oil our hands leave behind.	Our oil glands produce oil to help waterproof our skin.	Do this activity prior to activity #6, Don't Forget the Soap!, on page 17, to best reinforce this concept.	Make sure the cup is fresh from the package. This activity only works with a clean cup.

⑥ Don't Forget the Soap!

Did you know?
Soap holds onto the oil and microbes on our skin and then carries them down the drain with the water.

You will need
2 small see-through plastic bottles with lids (small empty water bottles work well)

2 cups water

2 drops blue food coloring

Measuring spoon

4 tablespoons liquid cooking oil

5 tablespoons liquid dishwashing detergent (Joy or green Dawn works well)

What do you think?
If I pour dishwashing detergent into a bottle filled with oil and water, it (will) or (won't) mix them together.

Now you are ready to
1. Fill each bottle with 1 cup of water. Drop 1 drop of blue food coloring into the water in each of the plastic bottles. This will allow you to identify the water.

2. Tightly fasten each bottle's lid, and shake.

3. Pour 2 tablespoons of liquid cooking oil into each of the plastic bottles. Replace the lids. Wait a minute and observe the liquid inside each bottle. What do you think happened to the bottle ingredients? Are the water and oil separating?

4. Open the lid to one of the bottles and pour in 5 tablespoons of dishwashing detergent. Tightly fasten the lid and shake vigorously. Does the bottle with the soap look the same or different than the bottle without the soap? What do you think is happening?

5. Shake both bottles at the same time. Put them down and watch what happens. Do they look the same or different? The bottle with oil and water will soon look the way it did in the beginning. Oil and water separate from each other. Soap brings oil and water together.

Brain exercise
When the soap was in the bottle with the oil and water in it, . . .

Activity Goal	Health Note	Key to Success	Hint
To see how soap brings oil and water together to help us clean our hands.	Washing with water alone does not clean our skin. The water just rolls over the oil. When soap is introduced, it brings the oil and water together so that the dirt can be washed off of our hands.	Do activity #5, Oily Me, Fingerprints Will Tell, page 16, before this activity so that the children have seen how oil collects on their skin.	The bottles used in this activity must be clean and have very tight lids.

7 Wash Enough? Do Your Hands Glow?

Did you know?
Microbes like to live on our hands. This is one way we spread the flu and other viruses.

You will need
Glo Germ cream (see product information, page 144)
Hands
Plenty of soap
Warm water
Ultraviolet lamp (see product information, page 144)
Hand towel(s)

What do you think?
If I thoroughly wash my hands as long as I usually do, I (will) or (won't) get the Glo Germ off my hands.

Now you are ready to
1. Rub the cream all over your hands. Remember to rub it in between each of your fingers and between your fingers and thumbs.
2. Wash your hands as thoroughly as you can with the soap and water. Remember to wash in between your fingers and between your fingers and thumbs. Germs love to hide there.
3. Go into a very dark room with an adult and see if you can see anything on your hands while looking at them with the ultraviolet lamp. If they aren't totally clean, you will be able to see fluorescent germs.
4. If you see anything, keep washing until your hands are free of color under the lamp.
5. When they are clean, dry your hands with the towel.

Brain exercise
When I looked under the ultraviolet lamp, . . .

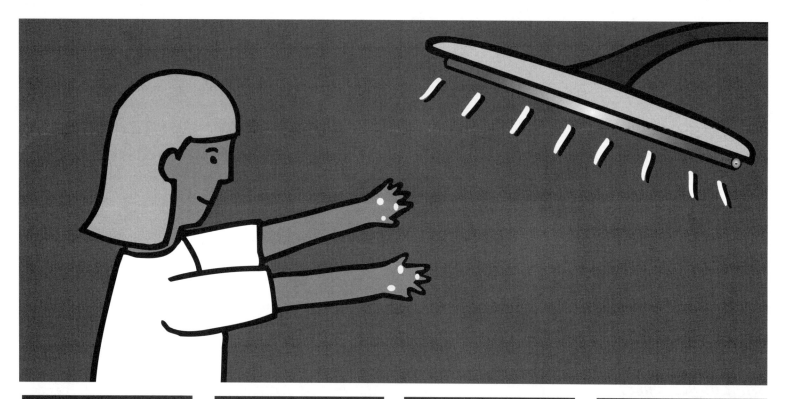

Activity Goal	Health Note	Key to Success	Hint
To view areas we miss when washing our hands.	Microorganisms love warm, moist environments. Our hands are the perfect vehicles for spreading disease. Drying is as important as washing our hands.	Model the proper way to wash hands before you start this activity. Talk about all of the ways we can get germs on our hands, including from our mouths, sneezes, and coughs.	The Glo Germ kit is relatively expensive for one family. However, it is well worth a school or multi-family purchase. If you have access to an ultraviolet lamp, the cream or powder alone are much more affordable.

⑧ Sing Along—Wash to Song

Did you know?

It takes about 30 seconds of good washing to get rid of the microbes on your hands.

You will need

Glo Germ Cream (see activity #7, Wash Enough? Do Your Hands Glow?, on page 19)

Your hands

Plenty of soap

Warm water

Your voice

Ultraviolet lamp

Hand towel(s)

What do you think?

If I wash my hands for as long as it takes me to sing *Happy Birthday to You* two times, I (will) or (won't) get all of the germs off my hands.

Now you are ready to

1. Rub the Glo Germ all over your hands. Remember to rub it in between each of your fingers and between your fingers and thumb.
2. Wash your hands as thoroughly as you can with the soap and water for as long as it takes you to sing *Happy Birthday to You* one time.
3. Go into a dark room with an adult and see if you can see anything on your hands while looking at them with the ultraviolet lamp.
4. If you see anything, wash your hands again as you sing *Happy Birthday to You* one more time.
5. Get your hands as dry as you can with the towel.

Brain exercise

From now on, when I wash my hands I am going to . . .

Activity Goal	Health Note	Key to Success	Hint
To teach children a familiar time frame for hand washing.	If we wash our hands while singing *Happy Birthday to You* two times, we will have removed most of the germs.	If you make this activity fun and festive, your children will continue to sing the song as they wash.	Keep plenty of small hand towels available.

⑨ Catch-a-Sneeze Chart and Award

Did you know?
A sneeze bursts out of your nose and mouth at speeds of up to 100 miles per hour.

You will need
Disposable tissues

Catch-a-Sneeze Chart, page 23, copied onto white paper (for individual children)

Large piece of butcher paper (for a class project)

Markers

Pencils

Catch-a-Sneeze Award, page 23, copied onto card stock and laminated

What do you think?
If I catch a sneeze, my germs (will) or (won't) infect other people.

Now you are ready to
1. Every time you sneeze, cover your nose and mouth with a tissue and catch that sneeze. Throw the tissue away immediately. Wash your hands. If you don't have a tissue, try catching the sneeze in the inside part of your elbow.
2. Record the sneeze you caught on the Catch-a-Sneeze Chart.
3. Keep the chart handy so that any time you catch a sneeze, you will be able to write it down.
4. At the end of a week, see how many sneezes you caught.
5. The person who caught the most sneezes will get the Catch-a-Sneeze Award for the week.

Brain exercise
When I caught my sneeze, I . . .

Activity Goal	Health Note	Key to Success	Hint
To practice and reinforce good hygiene.	An unprotected sneeze has the ability to travel 12 feet and sprays about 5,000 water droplets containing microbes into the air.	Make this a very fun and highly esteemed award. You and your students will benefit.	Children need to wash after a sneeze to get rid of residual germs.

Catch-a-Sneeze Chart and Award

Name	Sneezes Caught									
_____	☐	☐	☐	☐	☐	☐	☐	☐	☐	☐
_____	☐	☐	☐	☐	☐	☐	☐	☐	☐	☐
_____	☐	☐	☐	☐	☐	☐	☐	☐	☐	☐
_____	☐	☐	☐	☐	☐	☐	☐	☐	☐	☐
_____	☐	☐	☐	☐	☐	☐	☐	☐	☐	☐
_____	☐	☐	☐	☐	☐	☐	☐	☐	☐	☐
_____	☐	☐	☐	☐	☐	☐	☐	☐	☐	☐
_____	☐	☐	☐	☐	☐	☐	☐	☐	☐	☐
_____	☐	☐	☐	☐	☐	☐	☐	☐	☐	☐
_____	☐	☐	☐	☐	☐	☐	☐	☐	☐	☐
_____	☐	☐	☐	☐	☐	☐	☐	☐	☐	☐
_____	☐	☐	☐	☐	☐	☐	☐	☐	☐	☐
_____	☐	☐	☐	☐	☐	☐	☐	☐	☐	☐
_____	☐	☐	☐	☐	☐	☐	☐	☐	☐	☐
_____	☐	☐	☐	☐	☐	☐	☐	☐	☐	☐
_____	☐	☐	☐	☐	☐	☐	☐	☐	☐	☐

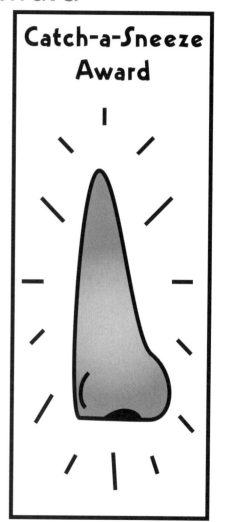

Catch-a-Sneeze Award

Healthy Me, © 1999. Published by Chicago Review Press, Inc., 800-888-7471.

Did you know?

When you cough, air droplets containing microbes rush out of your mouth at about 60 miles per hour.

You will need

Disposable tissue

What do you think?

If I cough against a tissue, it (will) or (won't) move away from me.

Now you are ready to

1. Hold the tissue by the top 2 corners about an inch in front of your mouth.
2. Cough into the tissue.
3. Did the tissue move when you coughed? If you were coughing your best cough, it should have moved. It is important to cover a cough and help keep others around you from getting any of your germs.

Brain exercise

When I covered my cough, I . . .

Activity Goal	Health Note	Key to Success	Hint
To practice and reinforce good hygiene.	If a tissue is not available, cover your mouth with the back of your hand. Wash your hands as often as you can.	The tissue needs to be close enough to the mouth to demonstrate the concept.	Although washing hands after covering a cough is not always convenient, it does decrease the spread of germs.

11 Grime Busters! Soap-Making Fun

You will need

1 bar (4 ounces) glycerin soap (unscented)

8-ounce glass measuring cup (or heavy saucepan if using a stove)

Microwave (or stove top)

11 drops lemon oil

1 drop yellow food coloring (optional)

Wooden spoon

Candy molds or empty ice cube trays (recycled)

Now you are ready to

1. Place the glycerin soap in the measuring cup or in a pan. Ask an adult to cook it on low heat in the microwave or on the stove, until it is totally melted (about 5 minutes).

2. Carefully take the cup out of the microwave.

3. Stir the lemon oil and food coloring into the melted glycerin soap with the wooden spoon.

4. Pour the soap mixture into fun-shaped candy molds.

5. Let the soap cool for 3 hours. Pop the soap out of the molds.

6. Use your lemon-scented soap the next time you wash your hands.

Activity Goal	Health Note	Key to Success	Hint
To promote hand washing.	Use unscented glycerin soap to limit any possible allergies.	Adult supervision is required. The microwave is the safest method of heating around children. It only takes a few minutes to melt the soap on low heat.	If you want to create other scents for soap, substitute the lemon oil with another fragrance such as cinnamon, lemon, or strawberry. This is a great gift idea for friends and relatives.

Great-Grandma's Shampoo Recipe

You will need

Tablespoon

1 bar castile soap (found in natural-food stores)

Cheese grater

Small bowl

3 cups water

Heavyweight saucepan

Stove top

Wooden spoon

11-ounce empty plastic shampoo bottle (recycled)

Now you are ready to

1. Carefully grate 8 tablespoons of the castile soap into the bowl.

2. Pour the water in the saucepan. Ask an adult to bring it to a boil and then to a simmer.

3. Pour the castile soap flakes into the saucepan. With the wooden spoon, stir the soap mixture until it is all dissolved.

4. Once the shampoo has cooled, pour it into the recycled bottle.

5. Use the shampoo when you wash your hair next time. Compare it to the other shampoos you've used.

Activity Goal	Health Note	Key to Success	Hint
To make and use an old-fashioned shampoo.	Buy unscented soap if children have allergies.	Children are surprised by the watery nature of this shampoo as compared to the thick shampoos used today. Make sure that the child testing the shampoo is prepared for the different consistency and that she closes her eyes before pouring it onto her hair.	Add drops of lemon oil for scent and one drop of yellow food coloring if desired for a more pleasant color.

⑬ Bountiful Bubbles—Make Your Own

Did you know?
A bubble is a very thin layer of soapy water wrapped around air.

You will need
Measuring cup

2 cups water

1-quart clean plastic bottle with lid

Funnel

2 ounces dishwashing detergent (Joy or green Dawn works well)

½ tablespoon glycerin (look in the drugstore skin-cream section)

Bubble blowers, page 29

Rectangular plastic dishwashing pan

Towel(s)

What do you think?
If I follow the bubble recipe, I (will) or (won't) make great bubbles.

Now you are ready to
1. Measure the water and pour it into the bottle, using the funnel.
2. Measure and pour the dishwashing detergent into the bottle.
3. Add glycerin to the soap mixture.
4. Put the lid tightly on the bottle and shake.
5. Pour the bubble mixture into the plastic pan.
6. Use the bubble blowers on page 29 to blow your bubbles.
7. When you are finished blowing bubbles, ask an adult to help you pour the rest of the mixture back into the bottle, using the funnel. You can save it for the next time you want to make bubbles.

Brain exercise
When I made bubbles, . . .

Activity Goal	**Health Note**	**Key to Success**	**Hint**
To make great bubbles with simple ingredients.	Make sure the children do not rub their eyes or drink the bubble water.	This can be a bit messy, but it is fun.	The glycerin is not a vital ingredient. However, it is the special ingredient that makes bubbles larger and stronger.

You will need

Thin, flexible wire

Duct tape

Scissors

Plastic strawberry container

Plastic straw with one end slit twice, flaps bent back

Plastic dishwashing pan containing the bubble mixture from page 27

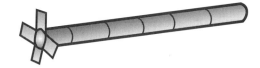

Now you are ready to

1. Bend the thin wire in half and wrap the ends together with duct tape to make a handle for the wand.

2. Make different shapes with the thin wire wand. Dip the wand into the bubble mixture and blow bubbles through it.

3. Dip the strawberry container into the bubble mixture and blow bubbles through it.

4. Dip the cut straw into the mixture. Blow from the uncut end and twist the straw to release the bubble.

5. Dip the wide end of the funnel into the bubble mixture and blow bubbles from the narrow end.

Activity Goal	Health Note	Key to Success	Hint
To create multiple bubble shapes with simple household items.	Make sure the children do not rub their eyes or drink the bubble water.	Each child should have access to at least one bubble blower.	Do this activity outside or in a work space prepared for water play.

⑮ Sponge It! Cleaning Art

You will need

Newspaper

Apron

1 package white tissue paper or classroom butcher paper

2 complementary colors water-based paint

2 empty cups

Sea sponge broken into small sections or small fun-shaped sponges

Small cup water

2 squares (4 x 4 inches) waxed paper

Now you are ready to

1. Place the newspaper out on a large, flat work space. Put on the apron.

2. If you are using tissue paper, make sure each wrapping piece is 3 layers thick to prevent the paint from bleeding through.

3. Pour small amounts of each paint color into separate cups.

4. Moisten 1 sponge by quickly dipping it into the water. Squeeze out any excess water. Gently dip it into the paint color of your choice. Do not soak the sponge.

5. Lightly touch the sponge to the tissue paper and lift it up again in a number of spots. Leave space for the other color. When finished, rest the sponge on the waxed paper.

6. Repeat steps 4 and 5 with the other color of paint.

Activity Goal	Health Note	Key to Success	Hint
To make beautiful wrapping paper with sponges.	Make sure children don't drink the paint.	Children must wear aprons. Preparing a work space for this activity ensures success.	Fun-shaped sponges are inexpensive and make designs that kids love.

Healthy Chompers

Sparkle, Sparkle, Pearly Whites

Sparkle, sparkle, pearly whites,
Make my smile shine big and bright.
Brush my chompers every day,
Floss to keep the plaque away,
Sparkle, sparkle, pearly whites,
Make my smile shine big and bright.

Sung to "Twinkle, Twinkle, Little Star"

TOOTH PASTE

FLOSS

In Healthy Chompers you will find

My Healthy Chompers Journal
Record your learning in pictures and words in your own special journal on page 34.

1. Indentations—Bite Your Teeth into an Apple
Are your toothprints unique? Find out on page 36.

2. Sugary Sweet? Not a Tooth Treat
What happens if you leave a tooth in cola? See for yourself on page 37.

3. Brush Enough? Plaque Test
Do you get all of the plaque off your teeth when you brush? Take the test on page 38.

4. Squeaky Clean—Listen and Brush
Can you sing your way to healthy teeth? Your chance to sing your heart out is on page 40.

5. Out of Toothpaste? Make Your Own
Have you ever made your own toothpaste? Learn the simple recipe on page 42.

6. Flavored Floss—Test the Taste
Which flavor of floss is your favorite? Do your own taste test on page 43.

7. Name-That-Tooth Book
Have you ever wondered what the names of your teeth are? To make a tooth book, flip to page 44.

8. I-Lost-a-Tooth Counting Chart
Do you remember when you lost your last tooth? Now you can record your lost teeth in a chart on page 46.

9. Catch a Falling Tooth—My Teeny Tiny Tooth Envelope
Do you have a place to put your teeth when they fall out? Don't wait another minute! Go make the envelope on page 49 right now, and save that tooth.

10. Make a Backpack Key Chain
Does your backpack need decorating? Make a key chain with your name on it out of ribbon floss, on page 50.

11. Dental Art
Would you like to paint with a toothbrush? Try out your dental tools on page 52.

12. Toothbrush Holder—Mold It Yourself
How would you like your own toothbrush holder? Make it yourself on page 53.

13. Magic Memories—A Special Smile Paper Quilt
What does your smile look like? Save your smile in a special quilt on page 55.

My Healthy Chompers Journal

Today I learned

White and Bright—Keeping Healthy Chompers

What should I know about healthy chompers?

✪ You will have two sets of teeth in your life. The first set is called your *milk teeth* or *baby teeth*. Pairs of milk teeth started to appear in your mouth when you were about seven months old. Your 20 milk teeth will fall out to make room for your 32 permanent teeth.

✪ At around six or seven years old, you will start getting permanent teeth, and you will probably have them all by the time you are 12.

✪ There are three different types of teeth: incisors, canines, and molars. The incisors slice and cut your food, while the canines are sharp and rip your food. The strong molars crush, chomp, and grind food to make it ready for you to swallow.

✪ You have two main parts to your teeth, the crowns and the roots. The pearly white crown is above your gums and the root is below. Gums are important because they keep your teeth in your mouth.

✪ The crowns of your teeth are covered with the hardest substance in your body, enamel. Enamel protects the nerves inside your tooth.

✪ When you eat, little bits of your food stay inside your mouth. They feed the bacteria that grow in a sticky filmy substance called *plaque*. Plaque attacks your tooth enamel and causes holes in your teeth, called *cavities*.

✪ Brushing your teeth after you eat gets rid of the food and the plaque. It is important to brush long enough to get your teeth squeaky clean (two minutes). Buying a new toothbrush every season (every three months) keeps your toothbrush fresh and keeps your teeth healthy. Your toothpaste should have fluoride in it to help fight cavities.

✪ Flossing your teeth removes the food that gets stuck in between your teeth and in other places your toothbrush can't reach.

✪ It is important to visit your dentist twice a year to make sure your teeth stay white, bright, and healthy.

Indentations—Bite Your Teeth into an Apple

Did you know?
Your toothprints are unique.

You will need
Apple slicer (optional but very functional)

Thick slice of a cored apple

Napkin

Plastic sandwich bag

Permanent marker

What do you think?
If I bite into an apple slice, my teeth (will) or (won't) make their own special prints.

Now you are ready to
1. Carefully bite into the inside of the apple slice. Take the remaining portion of the apple slice away from your mouth.
2. Place the bitten apple slice in the plastic sandwich bag. Use the napkin if it is messy.
3. Write your name on the bag with the permanent marker.
4. Compare your toothprints with those of others. Do they look the same? If not, what looks different?

Brain exercise
When I bit into the apple, my teeth . . .

Activity Goal	Health Note	Key to Success	Hint
To make a set of tooth-prints to compare with others.	Make sure the apple slices are kept in plastic bags. This will help limit the transmission of germs.	The apple slice needs to be big enough to actually record the upper and lower teeth pattern.	Using an apple slicer ensures the uniformity of each apple slice. The slices end up just the right size for this activity.

② Sugary Sweet? Not a Tooth Treat

Did you know?
Certain foods and drinks can cause cavities in your teeth.

You will need
Tooth
Small clear plastic cup of cola
Label
Pen

What do you think?
If I drop a tooth into a cup of cola, the tooth (will) or (won't) be affected by the cola.

Now you are ready to
1. Save a tooth that has fallen out of your mouth to make room for your permanent tooth.
2. Place the tooth in the small cup of cola. Write "tooth cup" on the label. Attach the label to the cup.
3. Keep the tooth in the cola for 1 week.
4. On the seventh day, check on the tooth. What happened to it? Why do you think that the tooth reacted this way?

Brain exercise
When my tooth sat in the cola, . . .

Activity Goal	Health Note	Key to Success	Hint
To see how cola affects tooth health.	Be sure to label the cup of cola as part of an experiment so no one will drink it. Most colas will eventually eat through the tooth enamel.	If children are concerned about the tooth fairy, ask them to leave the tooth fairy a note requesting the tooth back. This works very well.	Contact your local dentist if you can't find a tooth.

3 Brush Enough? Plaque Test

Did you know?
Plaque is the whitish-colored film that sticks to your teeth. It will turn a red color when you use a disclosing tablet.

You will need
Toothbrush
Toothpaste
Sink
Disclosing tablet (see product information, page 144)
Paper cup filled with water
Towel
Mirror

What do you think?
If I brush my teeth the way I usually do, I (will) or (won't) have any red left on my teeth after I chew the disclosing tablet.

Now you are ready to
1. Brush your teeth just the way that you usually do.
2. Chew the disclosing tablet and then spit it into the sink.
3. Take the cup filled with water and rinse out your mouth. Spit the water out. Dry your face and hands with the towel.
4. Check your teeth in the mirror. Do they have any red color left on them?
5. If your teeth have color left on them, this means you didn't get all of the plaque off them. Notice the places you've missed. You need to brush again, especially in those spots, to get all of that plaque off.

Brain exercise
When I brushed my teeth, . . .

Activity Goal	Health Note	Key to Success	Hint
To show where plaque is hiding.	Plaque is the major cause of tooth decay.	Model the proper way to brush teeth before you start this activity.	You might want to discuss the fact that, just as the germs on our hands can make us sick, the bacteria in plaque can harm our teeth.

4 Squeaky Clean—Listen and Brush

Did you know?
Most dentists recommend brushing for at least two minutes at a time. If your teeth squeak when you rub them, you know you did a good job in your brushing.

You will need
ABC song
Sparkle, Sparkle song, page 32
Battery-operated tape recorder
New cassette tape
Toothbrush
Toothpaste
Sink

What do you think?
If I brush my teeth while I listen to the ABC song and the Sparkle, Sparkle song, I (will) or (won't) get my teeth squeaky clean.

Now you are ready to
1. Sing the ABC and Sparkle, Sparkle songs once into the tape recorder and then once again. Rewind the tape.
2. Put the toothpaste on your toothbrush. Push the play button on the tape recorder and brush your teeth to the music. Brush the outside top teeth to the first ABC song, the inside top teeth to the Sparkle, Sparkle song, the outside bottom teeth to the second ABC song, and the inside bottom teeth to the second Sparkle, Sparkle song. Did you like brushing your teeth to your own music?
3. Check your teeth by rubbing them to see if they are squeaky clean.

Brain exercise
When I listened as I brushed, . . .

Activity Goal

To create a fun atmosphere in which children can brush their teeth.

Health Note

It is important to brush teeth long enough to adequately remove plaque and stimulate the gums.

Key to Success

Use only a battery-powered tape recorder. Ask children to practice recording their voices on a tape recorder ahead of time. This activity makes brushing fun.

Hint

Group singing works very well. Make a copy of the tape for each child to use at home.

You will need

Small paper cup

Measuring spoon

1 teaspoon baking soda

2 drops peppermint extract

3 drops water

Stirring spoon

Toothbrush

What do you think?

If I make my own toothpaste, it (will) or (won't) clean my teeth.

Now you are ready to

1. Mix the ingredients together in the paper cup.
2. Wet your toothbrush with water and then dip it into the toothpaste. Use the toothpaste to brush your teeth.
3. Do your teeth feel as clean as when you use your own toothpaste? Did you like the taste of this toothpaste?

Brain exercise

When I brushed my teeth with homemade toothpaste, . . .

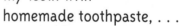

Activity Goal

To make a homemade toothpaste.

Health Note

This activity requires adult supervision. The recipe does not include fluoride. Fluoride helps fights cavities.

Hint

Some children like the taste of the baking soda toothpaste, while others do not like it at all. Using peppermint extract or another strong extract can help mask the salty soda taste.

6 Flavored Floss—Test the Taste

Did you know?

Flossing your teeth removes food from in between your teeth and other places your toothbrush can't reach.

You will need

Grape-flavored woven floss
Mint-flavored waxed floss
Bubble gum-flavored waxed floss

What do you think?

If I use floss to clean in between my teeth, it (will) or (won't) pull out bits of food.

Now you are ready to

1. Using a piece of grape-flavored floss, floss in between three of your teeth. Do you like the taste? Did anything come out with the floss?
2. Repeat step 1 with the mint- and bubble gum-flavored floss samples.
3. Which floss did you like the best?
4. Do you feel the floss helped you clean between your teeth?

Brain exercise

When I flossed my teeth, . . .

Activity Goals

To experience the benefits of flossing and to select a favorite floss.

Health Note

A lesson in the proper techniques for flossing needs to be done before this activity.

Key to Success

Make sure that there are a number of flavor options available to the children.

Hint

Try doing this activity after eating a meal so that the children can see first-hand the food that collects in teeth. Cinnamon is also an interesting floss flavor.

⑦ Name-That-Tooth Book

You will need

Name-That-Tooth Book, page 45, copied onto card stock

Scissors

Marker or crayon

Pencil

Now you are ready to

1. Cut out the oval book shape.
2. Fold the book in half on the dotted line so that when you open it up, you see the teeth inside.
3. Draw your face on the front cover and write your name on the back cover of your book.
4. Each time you lose a tooth, check inside your book to find the name of the tooth you lost. Color in each of your lost teeth with a crayon or marker.

Activity Goal	Health Note	Key to Success	Hint
To identify each milk tooth.	Learning the names and functions of their teeth helps children to understand their importance.	Children should keep the tooth book in a special place that is easily accessible.	The book can be placed with other important reference books or kept at the child's desk.

Name-That-Tooth Book

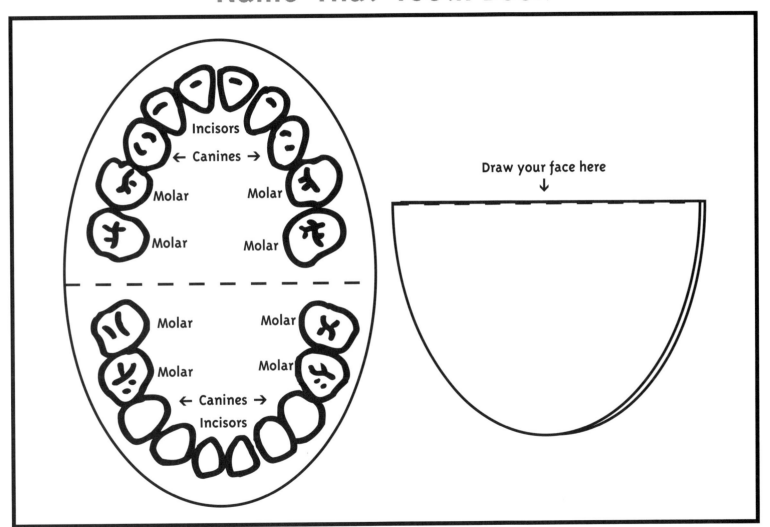

Incisors

← Canines →

Molar   Molar

Molar   Molar

Draw your face here
↓

Molar   Molar

Molar   Molar

← Canines →

Incisors

Healthy Me, © 1999. Published by Chicago Review Press, Inc., 800-888-7471.

8 I-Lost-a-Tooth Counting Chart

You will need

I-Lost-a-Tooth Counting Chart, page 47, copied onto card stock

Name-That-Tooth Book, page 45, copied onto card stock

Scissors

Pencil

Now you are ready to

1. Cut out the counting chart.
2. When a tooth falls out, locate it in your tooth book.
3. Write the date that each tooth fell out beside its number on the tooth counting chart.
4. Each time you lose a tooth, mark it down on your chart, and you will have a record of all your teeth.

Activity Goal

To record the date each tooth falls out.

Health Note

Each child will lose teeth at a different age. Reassure children who do not lose teeth as early as others that their teeth will fall out at just the right time for them.

Key to Success

Keep both the chart and the tooth book in a special place that is easily accessible.

Hint

The chart works well on a bulletin board or a refrigerator.

I-Lost-a-Tooth Counting Chart

1. _____
2. _____
3. _____
4. _____
5. _____
6. _____
7. _____
8. _____
9. _____
10. _____

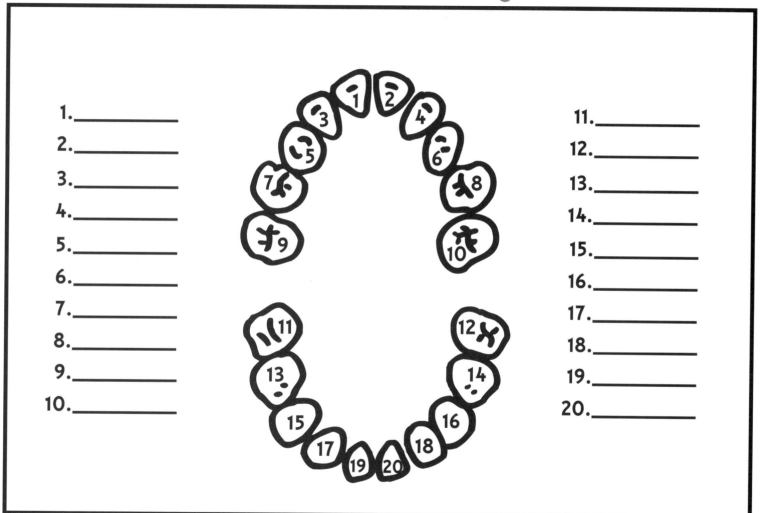

11. _____
12. _____
13. _____
14. _____
15. _____
16. _____
17. _____
18. _____
19. _____
20. _____

9 Catch a Falling Tooth—My Teeny Tiny Tooth Envelope

You will need

My Teeny Tiny Tooth envelope, page 49, copied onto a sheet of brightly colored paper

Scotch tape

Scissors

Post-it glue stick

Pencil or marker

Now you are ready to

1. Cut out the envelope shape.
2. Fold the bottom square behind the middle square. Tape the two squares together on both sides.
3. Fold the top piece behind the middle square to form an envelope shape. Tape the two sides together.
4. Use the removable glue stick on the back of the flap to keep it shut.
5. Write your name on the back of the envelope (the flap).
6. Save your teeny tiny tooth envelope for when your tooth falls out.

Activity Goal	Health Note	Key to Success	Hint
To make a special envelope to place teeth in as they fall out.	Save teeth for activity #2, Sugary Sweet? Not a Tooth Treat, page 37, to show how sugar can affect teeth.	Keep the envelope with the book on page 45 and the chart on page 47.	If the envelope is too small for little fingers, enlarge the diagram and use the enlargement for a template.

My Teeny Tiny Tooth Envelope

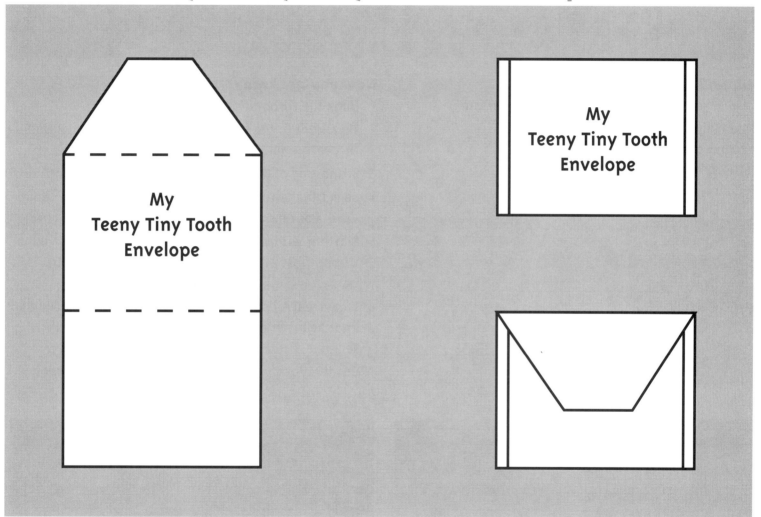

My
Teeny Tiny Tooth
Envelope

My
Teeny Tiny Tooth
Envelope

My
Teeny Tiny Tooth
Envelope

10 Make a Backpack Key Chain

You will need

11-inch piece ribbon floss (found in drugstores)
Small key ring
3 larger end beads
Letter beads (found in craft stores)
Scissors

Now you are ready to

1. Hook the ribbon floss around the key ring.
2. Tie a knot in the floss at the key ring to form 2 floss pieces of equal length.
3. String one of the larger end beads onto the floss.
4. Select the letter beads you need to write your name. Write your name with the beads.
5. Starting with the first letter of your name, weave the ribbon floss all the way to the last letter of your name.
6. Weave each floss piece through a large bead. Tie a knot at the end of the two beads to keep them secure.
7. Cut the floss at about an inch away from the knot.

Activity Goal	Health Note	Key to Success	Hint
To make a decorative key chain out of ribbon floss.	The more comfortable children are with handling floss, the more likely they are to use it on their teeth and gums.	Ribbon floss is the easiest type of floss to use for weaving beads. Beads need to have large enough openings to thread easily.	The chains are not strong enough to hold much weight. Children like attaching them to their backpacks for decoration.

My Backpack Key Chain

11 Dental Art

You will need

Apron

Construction paper

Newspaper

Old cleaned toothbrushes (one for each color of paint)

Different colors of tempera paint in small containers

Long pieces of different types of unused floss (waxed, woven, unwaxed)

Old clean rubber-tipped gum massager

Now you are ready to

1. Put on your apron.
2. Place the construction paper on top of the newspaper.
3. Carefully, dip a toothbrush in the paint and make a design on your paper.
4. Dip the floss and the gum massager in the paint and use them to make designs on your paper too.
5. How do you like painting with these silly paint-brushes?

Activity Goal	Health Note	Key to Success	Hint
To become more familiar and comfortable with handling dental tools.	This is a fun way to introduce new dental tools to children.	Adult supervision is necessary. Paint-filled toothbrushes can be very messy if they are not carefully monitored and aimed at paper only.	Using a small wire screen with a toothbrush and paint can make a very interesting design.

You will need

Apron
Measuring cup
Spoon
4 cups flour
1 cup salt
1½ cups water
Bowl
Rolling pin
Bottle opener
Empty frozen-juice can (no sharp edges)
Dull pencil (optional)
Cookie cutters (optional)
Cookie sheet
Oven
Paintbrush
Paints
Clear varnish spray

Now you are ready to

1. Put on the apron.
2. Pour the flour, salt, and water into the bowl. Stir until well blended.
3. Roll the flour mixture into a ball. Knead it for 5 to 10 minutes until it is smooth.
4. Roll out the dough you've formed to a ¼-inch thickness.
5. Use the bottle opener to make 2 holes in the bottom of the can for drainage.
6. Using the juice can sides as the shape, mold the dough around the outside of the can.
7. Try making different patterns on the dough. You could make a striped pattern with a dull pencil or write your name in the dough. Cookie cutter dough pieces pressed onto the molded dough are fun also.
8. Once you've finished molding your toothbrush holder, place it on the cookie sheet and bake in the oven at 250° for 2 hours.
9. Let the toothbrush holder dry. Then you can paint it and spray it with clear varnish.

Activity Goal	Health Note	Key to Success	Hint
To make tooth brushing even more special.	A toothbrush should be replaced every quarter (every three months).	If a child has a special place for his or her toothbrush, brushing becomes more fun. Adult supervision is necessary.	If you want to skip painting the toothbrush holder, add food coloring to your dough before baking.

13 Magic Memories—A Special Smile Paper Quilt

You will need

Camera

Photographs of big smiles showing lost teeth

Large sheet construction paper

Paper scraps: wrapping paper, wallpaper, construction paper, and newspaper

Glue

Now you are ready to

1. Take a picture of each child. Develop the pictures.
2. Use the sheet of construction paper to form the background for the quilt.
3. Use the paper scraps to make a picture frame for each child's picture.
4. Glue the pictures into the frames.
5. Glue the filled frames onto the construction-paper background.

Activity Goal	Health Note	Key to Success	Hint
To record toothless smiles in a wonderful paper quilt.	Children lose teeth at different ages. Full-teeth smiles are always welcome in smile quilts.	Kids need to smile for the camera.	Quarterly quilts are fun to make. They show how smiles change over time.

Nutritious and Delicious

I Love to Eat

I chomp up my proteins.
I eat veggies, too.
I love yogurt blizzards
From cows who say "moo."

I munch and crunch carbos.
I limit my sweets
To healthy, nutritious,
And tasty fruit treats.

Sung to "On Top of Old Smoky"

moo

In Nutritious and Delicious you will find

My Nutritious and Delicious Journal
Record your learning in pictures and words in your own special journal on page 60.

1. Nutrition Triorama
Do you know what foods you should be eating to stay healthy? To learn all about it, make the fun triorama on page 62.

2. Clean Your Treat Before You Eat?
Have you ever eaten unwashed veggies? See what's on them before they're washed, on page 64.

3. Fun Fruit—Itsy Bitsy Berry Bananas
Are you in the mood for a tangy treat? Check out page 65 for fun frozen fruit.

4. Fun Fruit—Naturally Sweet Fruit Cereal
Can you make your own healthy cereal? Follow the recipe on page 67 to make it yourself.

5. Dairy Delight—Yummy Yogurt 'n Fruit Blizzard
Does eating a blizzard sound interesting? Blend up a fruit-filled drink on page 69.

6. Dairy Delight—Build a Cottage Cheese Sundae
Would you like to build a nutritious sundae? Try page 71 for dairy fun.

7. Perfect Proteins—Make Your Own Peanut Butter and Almond Butter
Do you know how peanut butter is made? Learn the simple recipe and more on page 72.

8. Perfect Proteins—Deviled Egg Sailboats
Have you ever heard of an egg boat? Make your own and eat it, too, on page 74.

9. Crunchy Carbos—Single-Digit Pretzels
Are pretzels one of your favorite treats? Try shaping a number pretzel on page 76.

10. Crunchy Carbos—Ooey-Gooey Silly Sandwiches
Do you like sticky treats? If you do, the recipe on page 78 is the gooeyest.

11. Very Veggie—Ants on a Log
How would you like to eat something that looks like little ants on a log? If you are adventurous, try the log on page 79.

12. Very Veggie—Creative Cracker Spread
Are veggies your favorite food? They will be once you try the spread on page 80.

13. Quick and Healthy Snacks—Trail Mix
Have you ever eaten trail mix? Taste the recipe on page 81 for a new trail mix twist.

14. Quick and Healthy Snacks—Triple-Decker Mouthful
Do you have a big enough mouth to eat three layers? Stuff yourself on page 82.

15. Quick and Healthy Snacks—Frozen Grapes
Does your mouth need to cool down? Beat the heat with this cool treat on page 83.

 **My Nutritious and Delicious Journal**

Today I learned

Healthy Me, © 1999. Published by Chicago Review Press, Inc., 800-888-7471.

Eating Right—Staying Healthy

What should I know about nutrition?

✪ Just as a car needs gas to run, we all need food to fuel our bodies. Food contains the nutrients you need to grow and stay healthy. It gives you energy so that you can go through your day doing all of the amazing things that you do.

✪ You need to eat a variety of foods containing different vitamins and minerals in order to stay healthy.

✪ Foods like pasta, potatoes, rice, cereal, and bread are very important carbohydrates. Carbohydrates provide your body with energy.

✪ Vegetables contain lots of vitamins and minerals. Crunchy carrots give you vitamin A, tasty tomatoes give you vitamin C, and big-tree broccoli gives you vitamin K.

✪ Fruits are naturally sweet, delicious, and nutritious. They are full of important vitamins like vitamin C (oranges, strawberries, and watermelons).

✪ Foods like yogurt, milk, and cheese contain calcium, a mineral, that helps you grow big and strong. It keeps your teeth and bones healthy.

✪ Meats, eggs, fish, cheese, and nuts give you protein. Protein is very important in building muscle, skin, and bones.

✪ Some foods, like butter, cheese, cake, cookies, and chocolate, are high in fat. You only need to eat a small amount of fat every day to stay healthy. Too much fat is not good for your heart.

✪ Your body needs two to three quarts of water each day. Water can be found in the foods you eat as well as the things you drink.

1 Nutrition Triorama

You will need

Triorama design, page 63, copied onto white paper
Scissors
Colored pencils (optional)
Paste or glue stick

Now you are ready to

1. Cut out the triorama design. Color in the food drawings if you like.
2. Cut on the line between the empty triangle and the daily servings information.
3. Fold the daily serving triangle panel over the top of the empty triangular panel. Paste the two panels together.
4. Use your triorama when you plan your meals for the day.

Activity Goal	Health Note	Key to Success	Hint
To make a fun nutrition guide.	Fats, oils, and sweets are to be used sparingly.	Some children may need help with cutting and pasting.	Only cut up to the carbohydrate fold.

Nutrition Triorama

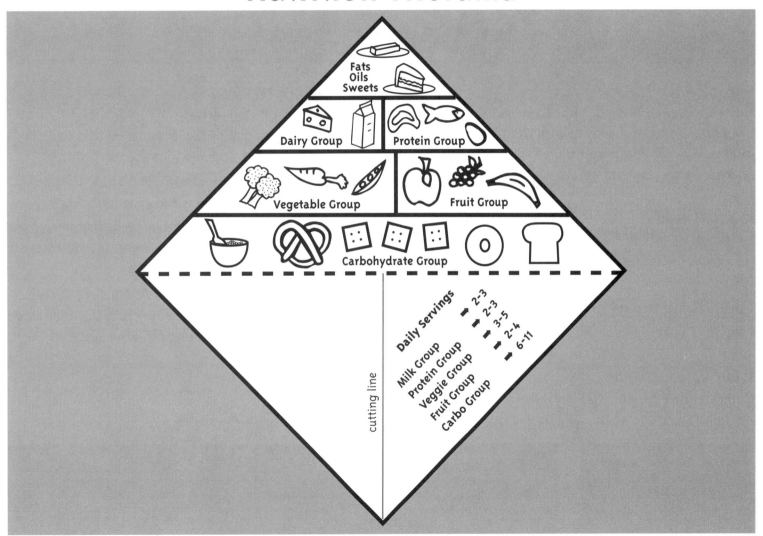

Fats
Oils
Sweets

Dairy Group

Protein Group

Vegetable Group

Fruit Group

Carbohydrate Group

cutting line

Daily Servings

Milk Group — 2-3
Protein Group — 2-3
Veggie Group — 3-5
Fruit Group — 2-4
Carbo Group — 6-11

Healthy Me, © 1999. Published by Chicago Review Press, Inc., 800-888-7471.

② Clean Your Treat Before You Eat?

Did you know?
Fruits and vegetables are shipped to us from all over the world. Some are sprayed with chemicals to keep the insects away. It is important to wash and clean the dirt and germs off our food before we eat it.

You will need
2 clean glass jars with lids
(like mayonnaise jars), recycled
Water
1 small carrot from the grocery store
Pen

What do you think?
If I place the carrot in a jar with water, the water (will) or (won't) be clean when I take the carrot out of the jar.

Now you are ready to
1. Fill each jar three-quarters full of fresh water.
2. Place the lid on one of the jars and set it aside.
3. Place the carrot into the remaining jar. Tightly secure the lid. Write a "C" on the lid of this jar.
4. Shake the carrot jar. What happens to the water?
5. Does the carrot water look the same as the other water? Describe how the water looks. Let the carrot sit in the jar for another 10 minutes.
6. Take the carrot out of the jar and shut the jar lid.
7. Compare the water inside the two jars. Is it the same or different? Which water would you want to drink? Why?

Brain exercise
The carrot made the water . . .

Activity Goal	Health Note	Key to Success	Hint
To demonstrate the importance of washing our food.	Nutritionists recommend washing all fruits (including bananas) and vegetables before they are eaten.	Glass jars work best for this activity. Make sure they are in a safe place to prevent breakage.	Buy the carrot individually rather than in a package.

③ Fun Fruit—Itsy Bitsy Berry Bananas

Makes approximately 20 individual pieces

You will need

¾ cup raspberries or strawberries (frozen fruit works well)

2 bananas, peeled and sliced into 10 pieces each

Measuring cup

Blender

Small mixing bowl

Spoon

Flat pan (cookie sheet or jelly-roll pan)

Waxed paper

Spatula

2 small freezer bags

Now you are ready to

1. Pour the berries into the blender. Blend them until the mixture is smooth.
2. Pour the berry mixture into the bowl. Drop the banana slices into the mixture.
3. Carefully, stir the bananas to cover them in the berry mixture.
4. Cover the flat pan with waxed paper. Using the spoon, place each dipped banana slice in its own spot on the waxed paper.
5. Place pan in the freezer for 10 minutes, or until bananas are slightly frozen.
6. Take the pan out of the freezer and use the spatula to place the banana slices in 2 small freezer bags or sandwich bags.
7. Freeze both bags.

Activity Goal

To taste a frozen fruit treat that is both nutritious and tasty.

Health Note

This recipe contains at least trace amounts of

Minerals	Vitamins
Calcium	A
Iron	B1
Magnesium	B2
Phosphorus	B3
Potassium	B6
Sodium	B9
Zinc	C
	E

Key to Success

Use a berry the children really like. Blackberries and raspberries work well. Don't leave the bananas in the freezer too long without protection, or they will get freezer burn.

Hint

Try inserting a Popsicle stick in a peeled banana half, dipping the banana in strawberry sauce, and freezing.

Fun Fruit—Naturally Sweet Fruit Cereal

You will need

2 apples
1 medium-ripe banana, peeled and sliced thin
1 teaspoon cinnamon
½ cup sliced almonds
1 cup raisins
½ cup grated coconut
2% milk (optional)
Cheese grater
Small mixing bowl
Measuring spoon
Measuring cup
Plastic spatula

Now you are ready to

1. Carefully grate the apples with a cheese grater positioned over the mixing bowl.
2. Add the banana slices to the grated apples in the mixing bowl.
3. Measure and add the cinnamon, sliced almonds, and raisins to the mixing bowl. Gently stir all of the ingredients together with the plastic spatula.
4. Measure the coconut and sprinkle it over the fruit mixture.
5. Enjoy this naturally sweet treat! You might try pouring milk over the top and eating it like cereal.

Activity Goal

To enjoy a nutritious alternative to breakfast cereal.

Health Note

This recipe contains at least trace amounts of

Minerals	Vitamins
Calcium	A
Iron	B_1
Magnesium	B_2

Key to Success

Apples will turn brown if grated too far in advance. Lemon juice will keep them fresh and more appetizing to the children.

Hint

If working with a large group, increase the recipe accordingly. Using a food processor to grate the apples makes increasing this recipe much easier, as does buying grated coconut. For a nutritious adventure, substitute multigrain milk or almond milk for 2% milk.

5 Dairy Delight—Yummy Yogurt 'n Fruit Blizzard

Makes approximately 4 cups

You will need

1 cup milk (2% works well)
½ cup vanilla yogurt
1¼ cups raspberries (frozen berries work well)
2 small ripe frozen bananas (peel before freezing)
1 teaspoon vanilla
Apron
Measuring cup
Blender
Measuring spoons
Paper cups

Now you are ready to

1. Put on the apron to protect your clothing.
2. Measure and pour both the milk and yogurt into the blender.
3. Measure the raspberries and pour them in the blender, too. Blend the mixture until it is smooth.
4. Break the frozen bananas into 4 or 5 pieces. Add them 1 piece at a time to the mixture and blend. Repeat until all pieces have been blended.
5. Add the vanilla and blend the mixture for about 30 seconds.
6. Pour yourself a delicious and nutritious blizzard!

Activity Goal

To make a delicious thick, frosty, and healthy drink.

Health Note

This recipe contains at least trace amounts of

Minerals	Vitamins
Calcium	A
Iron	B1
Magnesium	B2
Phosphorus	B3
Potassium	B6
Sodium	B9
Zinc	C
	E

Key to Success

Adult supervision is necessary. This recipe can be messy, and berries will stain clothing. Be sure to use aprons.

Hint

To make an even healthier drink, try using almond milk or multigrain milk (find these in health-food stores) in place of the 2% milk. They both are delicious in this recipe. If you are working with a large group, double the recipe and pour it into 2-ounce cups for taste testing.

6 Dairy Delight—Build a Cottage Cheese Sundae

You will need

¾ cup low-fat cottage cheese
½ cup pineapple chunks (canned)
¼ cup sliced strawberries
⅛ cup sliced almonds
Apron
Measuring cup(s)
Big spoon
Soup bowl
Butter knife

Now you are ready to

1. Put on the apron to protect your clothing.
2. Measure the cottage cheese and scoop it into the bowl.
3. Measure the pineapple chunks and scoop them into the cottage cheese.
4. Measure the strawberries and place them on top of the pineapple chunks.
5. Measure the almonds and sprinkle them onto the top of your sundae.

Activity Goal

To make a different yet delicious sundae.

° Health Note

This recipe contains at least trace amounts of

Minerals	Vitamins
Calcium	A
Iron	B1
Magnesium	B2
Phosphorus	B3
Potassium	B6
Sodium	B9
Zinc	C
	E

Key to Success

Adult supervision is necessary. Use only canned pineapple.

Hint

If you are working with a large group of children, try a taste-test version. Place small servings in paper cups using 1 spoonful cottage cheese, 3 pieces pineapple, 2 strawberry slices, and 1 almond slice. An assembly line with gloved hands is very efficient and fun.

You will need

Apron
Food processor or blender
Measuring spoons
Measuring cup
Containers with lids

Peanut Butter Recipe

2 cups shelled, roasted, unsalted peanuts
1 tablespoon peanut oil

or

Almond Butter Recipe

2 cups shelled, unsalted almonds (not blanched)
¼ tablespoon water or 1 tablespoon canola oil

Makes approximately 2 cups nut butter

Now you are ready to

1. Put on the apron to protect your clothing.
2. Measure the nuts and pour them into the food processor.
3. Measure the oil or water and pour it into the food processor.
4. Blend the nut mixture until it has a smooth consistency.
5. Refrigerate the nut butter in a sealed container. It will be good for about 1 week.

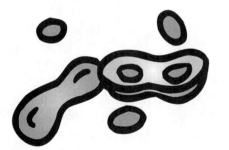
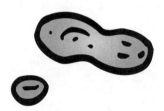

Activity Goal

To make your own peanut butter and try a more nutritious almond butter alternative.

Health Note

Peanut butter is higher in saturated fat than almond butter. This peanut butter recipe has no preservatives or additives. It is a healthier alternative than most commercial brands. This recipe contains at least trace amounts of

Minerals	Vitamins
Calcium	A
Iron	B1
Magnesium	B2
Phosphorus	B3
Potassium	B6
Sodium	B9
Zinc	C
	E

Key to Success

Adult supervision is necessary. Let children know ahead that the texture of almond butter is not as smooth as that of peanut butter.

Hint

If you are working with a large group of children, try a taste-test version. Increase the recipe accordingly and place small servings on soda crackers.

Perfect Proteins—Deviled Egg Sailboats

Makes enough for 2 egg sailboats

You will need

1 hard-boiled egg
1 teaspoon mayonnaise
½ teaspoon prepared mustard
Small bowl
Kitchen spoon
Knife (for adult use only)
2 copies of the sail on page 75
Scissors
Scotch tape
2 bright-colored toothpicks

Now you are ready to

1. Cut out the sail shapes. Tape the short side of each sail to a toothpick.
2. Remove the shell and cut the egg in half the long way. Take out the yolk. Place it in the bowl.
3. Add the mayonnaise and mustard to the egg yolk and mash them all together.
4. Using the spoon, fill the center cavity of the cooked egg white with the egg yolk mixture.
5. Stick your sail into the solid egg white in front of the filling. When ready to eat, pull the sail off and eat your deviled egg sailboat.

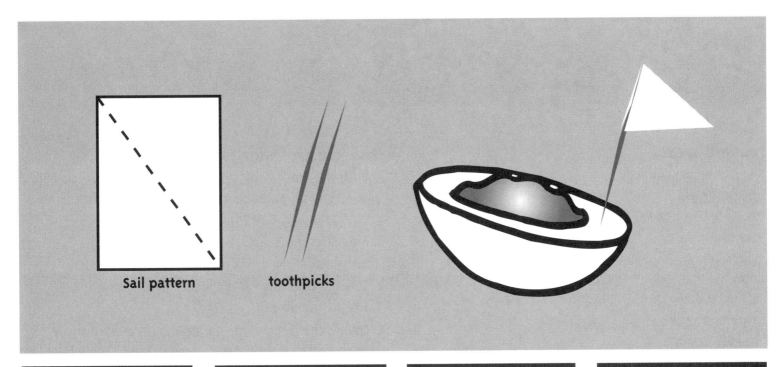

Sail pattern

toothpicks

Activity Goal

To make a fun protein treat.

Health Note

This recipe contains at least trace amounts of

Minerals	Vitamins
Calcium	A
Iron	B_1
Magnesium	B_2
Phosphorus	B_3
Potassium	B_6
Sodium	B_9
Zinc	C
	E

Key to Success

Place the sail in the solid egg white area.

Hint

Provide plenty of napkins for potentially messy, but fun, eating. Adult supervision is required with the toothpicks.

9 Crunchy Carbos—Single-Digit Pretzels

Makes approximately 12 medium pretzels

You will need

1½ cups warm water
1 package yeast
1 tablespoon honey
1 teaspoon salt
4 cups flour
1 egg
Salt in shaker
Large mixing bowl
Wooden spoon
Measuring spoons
Measuring cup
Cutting board sprinkled with flour
Greased cookie sheet
Egg beater
Pastry brush
Oven at 450°F

Now you are ready to

1. Pour the warm water into the mixing bowl. Sprinkle in the yeast and add the honey. Stir briefly and then let the mixture sit for about 5 minutes.

2. Measure and pour the salt and flour into the mixture.

3. Mix the dough with the wooden spoon and then knead the dough.

5. Divide the dough into small balls. Twist and turn each ball of dough into a snake shape.

5. Make a pretzel number out of your dough snake and place it on the greased cookie sheet. Try making a different number or shape out of each dough ball.

6. Use the egg beater to mix up the egg. Brush each pretzel with beaten egg and sprinkle each with salt.

7. Bake your pretzels for 12 to 15 minutes.

Activity Goal	Health Note	Key to Success	Hint
To make yummy pretzels.	This recipe contains at least trace amounts of	Check the yeast package date to ensure success.	Coarse salt makes these pretzels seem more like the kind you might find sold commercially. If you are working with a large group, allow each child to roll and twist his or her own ball of dough into a special shape.

Health Note

This recipe contains at least trace amounts of

Minerals	Vitamins
Calcium	A
Iron	B1
Magnesium	B2
Phosphorus	B3
Potassium	B6
Sodium	B9
Zinc	C
	E

10 Crunchy Carbos—Ooey-Gooey Silly Sandwiches

Makes 1 silly sandwich

You will need

2 graham cracker squares
1 tablespoon peanut butter (see recipe on page 72)
Honey in a squeeze bottle
Raisins or carob chips
Small spatula

Now you are ready to

1. Lay out the two crackers.

2. Gently spread a layer of peanut butter on top of one of the crackers. Write the first letter of your name in honey on top of the peanut butter.

3. For fun, add five raisins or five carob chips on top of the honey.

4. Gently place the remaining graham cracker on top of the other cracker to form a truly ooey-gooey silly sandwich.

Activity Goal	Health Note		Key to Success	Hint
To make fun and tasty sandwiches.	This recipe contains at least trace amounts of		Be careful with graham crackers. They will break if too much pressure is applied to them.	Try using the almond butter recipe as a substitute for the peanut butter.
	Minerals	Vitamins		
	Calcium	A		
	Iron	B1		
	Magnesium	B2		
	Phosphorus	B3		
	Potassium	B6		
	Sodium	B9		
	Zinc	C		
		E		

11 Very Veggie—Ants on a Log

Makes 8 small servings

You will need

8 small cleaned celery sticks

½ cup peanut butter or ½ cup almond butter (see recipes page 72)

¼ cup raisins or ¼ cup carob chips

Small spatula

Now you are ready to

1. Use the spatula to fill the inside curve of the celery with peanut butter or almond butter.

2. Place raisins or carob chips onto the peanut butter or almond butter.

3. Crunch into your yummy Ants on a Log.

Activity Goal	Health Note		Key to Success	Hint
To make eating vegetables fun.	This recipe contains at least trace amounts of		An adult should clean and cut the celery sticks before the activity begins.	The almond butter recipe tastes great with celery.
	Minerals	**Vitamins**		
	Calcium	A		
	Iron	B1		
	Magnesium	B2		
	Phosphorus	B3		
	Potassium	B6		
	Sodium	B9		
	Zinc	C		
		E		

12 Very Veggie—Creative Cracker Spread

Makes approximately ½ cup

You will need

1 cup raw shelled sunflower seeds (soaked in water for 2 hours)

½ cup roughly chopped fresh broccoli

½ cup roughly chopped fresh carrot

¼ cup roughly chopped fresh cilantro

1 tablespoon lemon juice

1 teaspoon salt

1 clove garlic

Blender or food processor

Now you are ready to

1. Combine all ingredients in a blender or food processor. Blend until semi-smooth.

2. Spread veggie mixture on a cracker or mini-rice cake.

3. Chomp away!

Activity Goal	Health Note		Key to Success	Hint
To make eating vegetables fun.	This recipe contains at least trace amounts of		Adult supervision is needed in using the blender or food processor.	Even children who claim to not like veggies like this yummy spread.
	Minerals	Vitamins		
	Calcium	A		
	Iron	B1		
	Magnesium	B2		
	Phosphorus	B3		
	Potassium	B6		
	Sodium	B9		
	Zinc	C		
		E		

⓭ Quick and Healthy Snacks—Trail Mix

You will need

¼ cup raisins or other dried fruit
½ cup Cheerios
¼ cup carob chips
½ cup shelled, unsalted almonds, not blanched
Large plastic food-storage bag
Individual sandwich bags

Now you are ready to

1. Pour all ingredients into the large plastic food-storage bag.
2. Seal the bag and shake it.
3. Pour the trail mix into individual sandwich bags.

Activity Goal	Health Note		Key to Success	Hint
To make a quick, healthy snack.	This recipe contains at least trace amounts of		Make sure the child's preferences are accounted for by substituting preferred ingredients.	Dried pineapple pieces and sweetened dried cranberries are great substitutes. The children especially like carob chips.
	Minerals	Vitamins		
	Calcium	A		
	Iron	B1		
	Magnesium	B2		
	Phosphorus	B3		
	Potassium	B6		
	Sodium	B9		
	Zinc	C		
		E		

You will need

3 tiny rice cakes
Peanut butter (recipe page 72)
Favorite jelly
Butter knife

Now you are ready to

1. Lay out the three rice cakes.
2. Spread peanut butter on the first rice cake.
3. Leave the second rice cake plain.
4. Spread jelly on the third rice cake.
5. Put the three rice cakes together to form a sandwich.
6. Open up wide and take a big triple-decker mouthful!

Activity Goal	Health Note	Key to Success	Hint
To make a quick, healthy snack.	This recipe contains at least trace amounts of Minerals — Vitamins Calcium — A Iron — B1 Magnesium — B2 Phosphorus — B3 Potassium — B6 Sodium — B9 Zinc — C — E	Use the flattest side of the rice cakes on the inside of the sandwich.	This is a fun recipe for school snacks. Because it is a tasty mouthful, the children love it.

Quick and Healthy Snacks—Frozen Grapes

You will need
Bunch of fresh grapes
Individual sandwich bags
Freezer

Now you are ready to
1. Carefully clean and wash the grapes.
2. Remove all stems.
3. Place a number of grapes in each sandwich bag and freeze for a fast treat on a hot day.

Activity Goal	Health Note		Key to Success	Hint
To make a quick, healthy snack.	This recipe contains at least trace amounts of		Use the sweetest grapes available. Always wash before you freeze.	Try dipping the grapes in the berry puree on page 65 and freezing for a tangy treat.
	Minerals	Vitamins		
	Calcium	A		
	Iron	B1		
	Magnesium	B2		
	Phosphorus	B3		
	Potassium	B6		
	Sodium	B9		
	Zinc	C		
		E		

Exercising My Muscles

I Exercise Each Day

I eat right and I am strong!
I exercise each day.
I train my muscles so that they
Work for me when I play!
Exercising—that's for me.
Muscles come in handy.
I'll build my muscles big and strong
So they will work just dandy.

Sung to "Yankee Doodle"

In Exercising My Muscles you will find

My Exercising Journal

Today I learned

Exercising My Muscles—Staying Healthy

What should I know about exercising?

✪ Exercise helps to keep your mind and body healthy.

✪ Almost half your body weight comes from the muscles in your body.

✪ When you exercise, you build strong muscles. The more you use your muscles, the stronger they become.

✪ Aerobic exercises like swimming, biking, and running help to keep your heart strong and healthy. Your heart is the strongest muscle in your body. It has to be a very powerful muscle to pump blood around your body. You can feel it pumping in your wrist, neck, and chest. This is called your *pulse*. The number of times your heart beats in one minute is called a *pulse rate*. Your pulse rate is higher than your parents'. It is also true that a person's heart beats faster during exercise than during rest. When your heart beats faster, your pulse rate speeds up.

✪ When your body heats up from exercising, water comes up through your skin as sweat to cool you down. It is important to drink plenty of water when you exercise so that you will replace the water you are losing through sweat.

✪ Muscles need to be warmed up before they are used to do work. Always stretch first and then do your exercise. After you are finished exercising, make sure that you give your muscles time to cool down and relax.

✪ Scientists have found that when you exercise, your body releases chemicals called *endorphins*. Endorphins create a happy feeling in your brain.

① Wet Sweat—Time to Cool Off?

Did you know?
Sweat is mainly made up of water. We sweat to cool off on hot days or when we exercise.

You will need
Your hand
Your tongue or a wet cotton ball

What do you think?
If I wet the back of my hand, my skin (will) or (won't) feel cool when I blow air across it.

Now you are ready to
1. Raise the back of your hand up to your mouth and gently blow air across it. How does it feel? Does it tickle? Does it feel warm or cool?

2. Wet the back of your hand by using a wet cotton ball or just by licking it. Gently blow air across it. How does it feel? Does it tickle? Does it feel warm or cool?

Brain exercise
My breath made my wet hand . . .

Activity Goal	Health Note	Key to Success	Hint
To simulate the effect that sweat has in cooling our bodies down.	We lose water when we sweat. It is important to replenish this water, especially after exercise.	Air needs to be blown across the hand before the water has evaporated.	Wet paper towels, wipes, or running water will all produce the same effect.

② Magnificent Muscles—Cold or Warm?

Did you know?
Your muscles need to warm up before they do work.

You will need
Small, individually wrapped Tootsie Roll, chilled, or saltwater taffy, chilled
Warm hands

What do you think?
If I try to stretch a cold Tootsie Roll, it (will) or (won't) be flexible.

Now you are ready to
1. Take the cold Tootsie Roll and try to make it stretch. Does it stretch very well?
2. Hold the Tootsie Roll with both hands. Is it warming up? What do you notice as it warms up?
3. Once the Tootsie Roll is warm, try stretching it again. Does it stretch more easily now? How is the Tootsie Roll like your muscles? Do you think it is important to warm up your muscles? Our muscles are much more flexible when they are warmed up before we use them.

Brain exercise
When I tried to stretch a cold Tootsie Roll, it . . .

Activity Goal	Health Note	Key to Success	Hint
To introduce the concept of flexibility and stretching.	Even children need to warm up their muscles before they do strenuous exercise.	Make sure the Tootsie Rolls or taffy pieces are cold before starting this activity.	If you prefer using a nonfood item, try using modeling clay instead of Tootsie Rolls or saltwater taffy.

③ Silly Stretch Activity

Did you know?
It is important always to stretch before and after exercise.

You will need
8 pieces white card stock cut into 8-inch squares (These can be laminated after the drawings are completed.)
Markers
Silly Stretch poem, page 93
Adult
Partner(s) are optional

What do you think?
If I listen to the Silly Stretch poem and stretch my muscles, I (will) or (won't) be ready to exercise.

Now you are ready to
1. Draw a big picture of toes on the first piece of card stock. Label it **#1**.
2. Draw a big picture of a nose on the second piece of card stock. Label it **#2**.
3. Draw a big picture of a sun on the third piece of card stock. Label it **#3**.
4. Draw a big picture of marching feet on the fourth piece of card stock. Label it **#4**.
5. Draw a big picture of flying wings on the fifth piece of card stock. Label it **#5**.
6. Draw a big picture of an arrow bending left on the sixth piece of card stock. Label it **#6**.
7. Draw a big picture of an arrow bending right on the seventh piece of card stock. Label it **#7**.
8. Draw a big picture of an arrow circling up to the sky on the eighth piece of card stock. Label it **#8**.
9. Ask someone to read the Silly Stretch poem and hold up the cards while you follow along.
10. When you are finished, you will be all ready to exercise.

Brain exercise
When I followed the Silly Stretch poem, . . .

Silly Stretch Poem

Touch your toes
And touch your nose.
Reach up to the sky!

Start marching
And flap your wings.
Pretend that you can fly!

Bend to your left
And to your right.
Swing your arms up high!

Now touch your toes
And touch your nose.
Reach up to the sky!

Activity Goal	Health Note	Key to Success	Hint
To introduce the concept of stretching.	It is important for children to make stretching part of their exercise routines.	Make sure there is plenty of room for movement without violating someone else's space requirements.	Ask children to help draw the pictures. If you have no budding artists, try using magazine pictures.

④ Time to Take a Water Break!

Did you know?

When your body heats up from exercising, water comes up through your skin as sweat to cool you down. It is important to drink plenty of water when you exercise so that you will replace the water you are losing through sweat.

You will need

Thumbs Up for Water sheet, page 96, copied onto card stock
Exercise gear for whatever sport you choose
Cool water in a water bottle
Clock

What do you think?

If I follow the Thumbs Up for Water sheet, I (will) or (won't) have a dry mouth.

Now you are ready to

1. Choose the team sport you want to play with your friends.
2. Drink about 1½ cups of cool water 2 hours before you play the sport you've chosen.
3. Drink a cup of cool water 15 minutes before you play.
4. Take your water bottle filled with cool water to the game with you. Take a drink at least every 15 minutes.
5. After you've finished playing, be sure and drink a cup or two of cool water to replenish the water you've lost through sweating.

Brain exercise

When I play sports, I need water to . . .

Thumbs Up for Water

Exercise and Water

A Perfect Match

2 hours before

During exercise

15 minutes before

Right after

or

Healthy Me, © 1999. Published by Chicago Review Press, Inc., 800-888-7471.

Activity Goal

To identify the amount of water lost when exercising, and to replace it.

Health Note

If children don't drink enough water while playing sports, they can become dehydrated. One symptom of dehydration is a dry mouth. When it is hot, there is a higher risk for heat exhaustion.

Key to Success

Keep the Thumbs Up for Water sheet in a spot where children can see it before they play a sport.

Hint

Always have a fresh water bottle in the refrigerator.

⑤ March to the Music

Did you know?
When you exercise, your heart beats faster than when you are resting.

You will need
The 8 drawings from activity #3, Silly Stretch, page 92
Silly Stretch poem, page 93
Timer
Partner
Tape or CD player
John Philip Sousa tape or CD of marches

What do you think?
If I exercise, my heart (will) or (won't) beat faster than it did before I exercised.

Now you are ready to
1. Put your hand over your heart. Can you feel it beating?
2. Use the Silly Stretch Activity, page 92, to warm up before your marching exercise.
3. Set the timer for 10 minutes. Turn on the marching music and start marching.
4. When the timer goes off, stop marching and put your hand over your heart again. Does it feel the same or faster than before?

Brain exercise
After I marched, my heart . . .

Activity Goal	Health Note	Key to Success	Hint
To see the difference between your heart at rest and your heart after exercise.	Ask children to place their hands across their hearts as they do when they say the Pledge of Allegiance.	Finding marching music that kids really enjoy.	It's fun to follow a leader in this activity. Try to march like a band, where everyone steps on the same beat.

6 Pathways—Healthy and Not-So-Healthy Choices

Did you know?
Every time you choose a healthy food to eat, you are giving your body energy to build your muscles.

You will need
10 laminated cards picturing a variety of foods, some healthy and some not-so-healthy (magazine photographs work well)

Space large enough for all children to move about freely

Adult or leader

What do you think?
If I see a card with a certain food on it, I (will) or (won't) be able to tell if it is a healthy food.

Now you are ready to
1. Talk about foods that are healthy (for example, fruits and vegetables) and not-so-healthy (candy, potato chips).
2. Get on the opposite side of the room from the leader or adult. The leader will hold up a picture of food. If the leader holds up a card that has a picture of a healthy food, walk straight to the other side of the room. If the leader holds up a card that has a picture of not-so-healthy food, walk in a small zigzag pattern to the other side of the room.
3. Check out your answer with the leader. Do you agree that the food in the picture is healthy or not-so-healthy? Discuss your answer.

Brain exercise
When I saw not-so-healthy food, I . . .

Activity Goals	Health Note	Key to Success	Hint
To travel in two different pathways (zigzag and straight). To identify healthy and not-so-healthy foods.	It is important for children to start identifying nutritious foods so that they can make informed food choices.	Select an area like a gym, garage, or playing field that has plenty of room for children to move about freely.	Cut pictures of food from magazine or newspaper advertising, or use clip art to make the laminated food cards.

7 Kids Like to Move—Can Project

You will need

Permanent marker
4 red Popsicle or craft sticks
4 blue Popsicle or craft sticks
3 green Popsicle or craft sticks
3 yellow Popsicle or craft sticks
Small safe juice can (no sharp edges)
Fun stickers

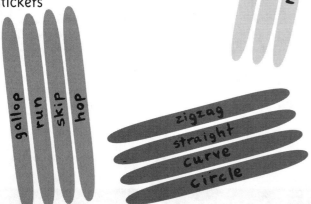

Now you are ready to

1. Use the permanent marker to label the red sticks with the names of exercise skills: gallop, run, skip, hop.
2. Label the blue sticks with the names of exercise pathways: zigzag, straight, curve, circle.
3. Label the green sticks with different exercise levels: high, low, medium.
4. Label the yellow sticks with different speeds: fast, slow, medium.
5. Decorate your can with fun stickers and label it "Moving!" Put the labeled sticks in the can.
6. You are now ready to do activity 8, page 101.

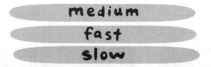

Activity Goal	Health Note	Key to Success	Hint
To get materials ready for activity #8—Simon Says Choose Your Move, page 101.	Keep the colored sticks out of mouths.	Let many children contribute in decorating the can.	Discuss the meaning of each colored stick with the children.

8 Simon Says Choose Your Move

You will need

Kids Like to Move can,
page 100

Labeled Popsicle or
craft sticks, page 100

A large running space
(like a gym or empty garage)

Now you are ready to

1. Choose 1 red stick. This will be your exercise skill.
2. Choose 1 blue stick. This will be your exercise pathway.
3. Choose 1 green stick. This will be your exercise level.
4. Choose 1 yellow stick. This will be your speed limit!
5. Select a starting place and an ending place. Then have a leader say, "One, two, three—GO!"
6. Repeat steps 1–5 to try a new pattern.

Activity Goal	Health Note	Key to Success	Hint
To incorporate different skills, pathways, levels, and speeds into a fun activity.	Simon Says allows children to train muscles they will need to use in the sports they are playing and will play in the future.	This activity works well with a large space like a school gym, playground, or park.	If you are working with a large group, ask different children to choose each of the sticks. The children love this activity. You can also discuss the concept of choosing randomly.

Did you know?

Walking is one of the best exercises. Walking is good for your heart as well as your muscles.

You will need

Your legs
An adult
A fun destination

What do you think?

If I go for a walk, I (will) or (won't) be getting good exercise.

Now you are ready to

1. Think about a wonderful place in nature. This might be a local park, zoo, or your own neighborhood.
2. Decide where you would like to go and ask an adult to go with you.
3. Walk together and talk about the things you see, hear, and smell in nature for about 20 minutes. That is enough time to give your heart a nice workout.
4. Think about other places you might like to go and explore in the next walk.

Brain exercise

When I went for a walk in nature, my muscles . . .

Activity Goal	Health Note	Key to Success	Hint
To start a habit of taking walks.	Walking is good for both adults and children. It is an aerobic exercise.	Children need to have the appropriate clothing and shoes for the weather and terrain.	An adult guide who enjoys walking and nature can inspire lifelong walkers. Many places have short hike guides for hiking with kids. If this sounds interesting, check it out at your local library or bookstore.

Did you know?
Dancing is a great form of exercise. It is fun and it works your heart and your muscles, too.

You will need
Your legs
Tape or CD player
Music selection from a familiar movie
Large space for dancing

What do you think?
If I dance, my heart (will) or (won't) be getting a good workout.

Now you are ready to
1. Find music that all of the dancers will enjoy. If you have many dancers, you might want to take a vote. Stretch before you start dancing.
2. Turn on your tape or CD player.
3. You can dance however you would like. Make sure you have enough space so that you do not run into another dancer. Dance to the music for about 15 minutes or longer, if you like. That is enough time to give your heart a nice workout. Each song will have its own special beat. Some will be faster than others. That is OK—just keep dancing.
4. Put your hand over your heart when you are finished dancing. Can you feel your heartbeat? Does it feel like your heart got a good workout?

Brain exercise
When I danced, my heart . . .

Activity Goals

To move to music and do aerobic exercise.

Health Note

Dancing is another aerobic exercise that is good for the heart and other muscles.

Key to Success

Find music that the children really enjoy. Many of the Disney movies have familiar music that the children love.

Hint

The dancing space needs to be large enough to avoid collisions. To hear a heartbeat, place an empty toilet paper roll over clothing next to the heart of a partner.

⑪ Beautiful Biceps

Did you know?
Your biceps are powerful muscles located in your upper arms. The more you exercise your biceps, the larger and more powerful they will become.

You will need
Index card
Pencil
Your arms
Partner
Cloth tape measure

What do you think?
If I measure each of my biceps, they (will) or (won't) be the same size.

Now you are ready to
1. Take the index card and draw a line down the middle. Now you have a left side and a right side.
2. Think about your arms. Do you use one arm more than the other? Do you think one arm's biceps will be bigger than another? If yes, which one do you predict will be bigger? Ask your partner to measure your left biceps with the cloth tape measure as you make a fist and show off your muscle as if you were a bodybuilder. Write the number of inches measured on your index card in the left column.
3. Ask your partner to measure your right arm as you make a fist and show off your muscle as if you were a bodybuilder. Write the number of inches measured on your index card in the right column.
4. Was there a difference between your two biceps? Was your prediction correct?
5. Now it's your turn to measure your partner's biceps by following steps 1–3.
6. Measure your biceps later in a couple of months to see if they are getting bigger.

Brain exercise
When I measured my partner's biceps, I . . .

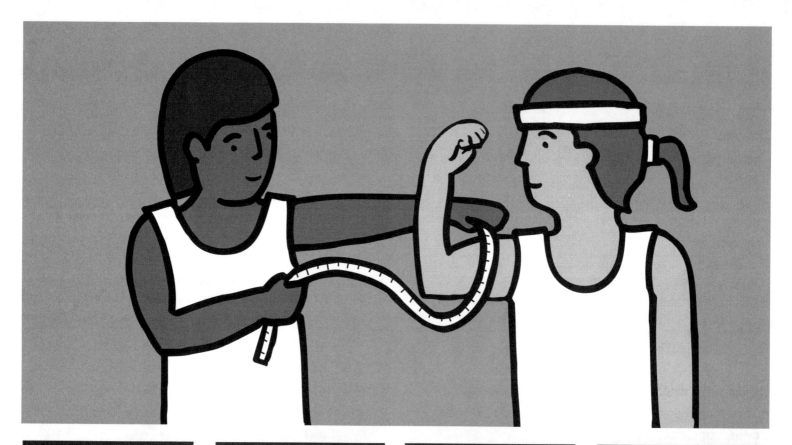

Activity Goal

To see how usage affects muscle size.

Health Note

The arm that is used most often will probably have the larger muscle.

Key to Success

Teach children how to read and use a tape measure in a mini-lesson before this activity.

Hint

Make sure the tape measure is soft and doesn't hurt the child's arm. Soft tape measures are very inexpensive and can be found at any fabric store.

12 Train Your Muscles

Did you know?
Your muscles come in many different sizes. You use small muscles when you write your name.

You will need
Pencil
Lined paper
Your hands

What do you think?
If I practice writing my name with the hand opposite to the one I usually use, I (will) or (won't) be able to improve my writing.

Now you are ready to
1. Write your name as you usually do at the top of your paper.
2. Try writing your name with your other hand on the first line.
3. Practice writing your name with your other hand every day. Write underneath the name you wrote the day before.
4. After 7 days, look at your writing. Has it improved?

Brain exercise
After I practiced writing with my other hand, my writing . . .

Activity Goal	Health Note	Key to Success	Hint
To train new muscles.	Fine motor skills are developed with use.	Ask children to practice every day.	Try doing this yourself. Show the children your writing.

⑬ Exercise Bingo I—Choices at Home

Did you know?

There are many different ways to exercise your muscles. You can play games with your friends or exercise by riding your bike all by yourself.

You will need

Exercise Bingo Board I, page 109, copied onto card stock
Partner (optional)
Bottle caps

What do you think?

If I exercise by doing some of the activities on the Bingo Board, I (will) or (won't) be able to make a bingo.

Now you are ready to

1. Look at the Bingo Board. Which exercise would you like to try first?
2. Find a friend or do the activity by yourself.
3. Once you have completed the activity, place a bottle cap on the symbol that represents it on the Bingo Board.
4. Each day when you come home from school, try doing a different activity.
5. Soon you will have a bingo.

Brain exercise

When I did the activities on the Bingo Board, I . . .

Activity Goal	Health Note	Key to Success	Hint
To try out a variety of fun exercise activities.	Most exercise activities require some protective gear like a helmet for a bicycle or a helmet and knee pads for roller blades. Adult supervision is required for some activities, like swimming.	Appropriate exercise equipment and protective gear make it possible for children to be successful at these activities.	Most YMCAs and Boys and Girls Clubs have equipment available and provide supervision for the children.

Exercise Bingo Board 1

Free Choice

14 Exercise Bingo II—Choices at School

Did you know?
Exercising every day builds strong muscles.

You will need
Exercise Bingo Board II, page 111, copied onto card stock

Partner (optional)

Bottle caps

What do you think?
If I exercise by doing some of the activities on the Bingo Board, I (will) or (won't) be able to make a bingo.

Now you are ready to
1. Look at the Bingo Board. Which exercise activity would you like to try first?
2. Find a friend or do the activity by yourself.
3. Once you have completed the activity, place a bottle cap on the symbol that represents that activity on the Bingo Board.
4. Each day you go to school, try doing a different activity.
5. See who gets the first bingo in your class.

Brain exercise
When I did the activities on the Bingo Board, I . . .

Activity Goal	Health Note	Key to Success	Hint
To try out a variety of fun exercise activities.	Most of the exercise activities on this Bingo Board do not require protective gear. However, in soccer, shin guards are required.	Make sure your school has equipment for these activities. Make your own Bingo Boards. If it doesn't, make up a Bingo Board for what your school has.	Most schools have all of the gear needed to create a bingo on this sheet.

Exercise Bingo Board II

⑮ Exercise Bingo III—Sports Bingo

Did you know?
You can strengthen many muscles by trying new sports or activities.

You will need
Exercise Bingo Board III, page 113, copied onto card stock

Partner (optional)

Bottle caps

What do you think?
If I exercise by doing some of the activities on the Bingo Board, I (will) or (won't) be able to make a bingo.

Now you are ready to
1. Look at the Bingo Board. Which sport would you like to try first?
2. Find a friend or do the activity by yourself.
3. Once you have completed the activity, place a bottle cap on the symbol that represents that activity on the Bingo Board.
4. Each weekend, try doing a different activity.
5. Soon you will have a bingo.

Brain exercise
When I did the activities on the Bingo Board, I . . .

Activity Goal	Health Note	Key to Success	Hint
To try out a variety of sports activities.	Most exercise activities require some protective gear like helmets or shin guards. Adult supervision is required for many of the Bingo Board III activities.	Appropriate exercise equipment and protective gear make it possible for children to be successful at these sports.	Adult participation in the sports makes them doubly fun for the children.

Exercise Bingo Board III

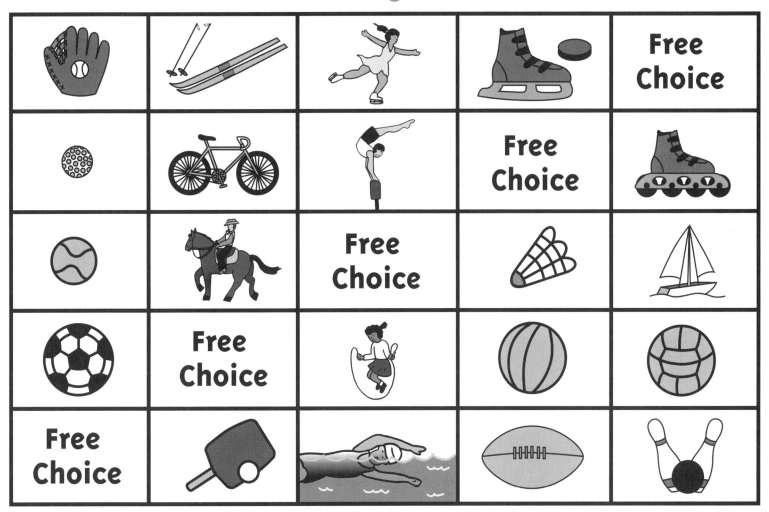

Safe and Sound

I Play It Safe

I know my address and phone, too!
I can repeat them back to you.
I know how to dial 911.
In emergencies I know what's done.

I wear my seat belt in the car
Even if we're not going far.
I wear a helmet riding my bike—
It has colors that I like!

Sung to "I'm a Little Teapot"

In Safe and Sound you will find

My Safe and Sound Journal
Record your learning in pictures and words in your own special journal on page 118.

1. In the Know—Know Your Numbers!
Do you know your name, address, and phone number? To learn a way to never forget them, turn to page 120.

2. Telephone Booth—A Field Trip
Have you ever dialed a number from a telephone booth? Push 0 for operator on page 122 and learn what to do if you need help.

3. Dial 911
Can you dial 911 if you need to get help? Learn how you can practice 911 so that you'll know what to do in an emergency, on page 124.

4. Make an Emergency Magnet
Does everyone in your family know the emergency number? Make a fun magnet to put up on your refrigerator, on page 125.

5. Check It Out—Find the Exits
Where are the exits at the grocery store? Use your detective skills to learn where exits are at your favorite places, on page 127.

6. Safety Belts—Buckle Up
Why do people wear safety belts? See for yourself on page 129.

7. Handy Helmet—Happy Head
What does a helmet do for your head in a crash? Find out in the activity on page 130.

8. Perfect Fit—Try It On!
Does your helmet fit properly? Check out your helmet on page 132.

9. Safety Signs
How many safety signs do you know? Test your knowledge on page 133.

10. Look Both Ways Song
Can you sing "Are You Sleeping?" If you can, then you will love singing about looking both ways, on page 135.

11. Buddy Up!—My Poster
Is drawing one of your favorite things to do? Use your markers and your imagination to create a fun poster on page 137.

12. Fill It Out and Pack It—Emergency Numbers
Do you carry a backpack? Ask an adult to help you fill out your emergency numbers, on page 138, and pack them with you for safekeeping.

13. Safe and Sound Kids—Safety Certificate
Have you done the activities in this chapter? If you have, you qualify for the special safety certificate on page 140.

My Safe and Sound Journal

Today I learned

Keeping Safe—Staying Healthy

What should I know about keeping safe and sound?

✪ Dialing 911 could save your life or the life of another person.

✪ Medical experts report that most bicyclists hurt in accidents were not wearing helmets. Helmets and bicycles go together. Make sure your helmet is adjusted just right for your head. Bicycle falls are the main cause of head injuries in kids.

✪ It's important to know your name, address, and phone number in case you ever get lost.

✪ You can always dial 0 from a phone booth if you are lost or need help. You don't have to have money to dial 0.

✪ Identifying building exits ahead of time will help you leave the building in an emergency.

✪ You should always wear your safety belt. Buckling up saves lives every day.

✪ Safety signs help us identify what is safe and what isn't safe.

✪ It is important to know where you can find a list of your emergency numbers.

In the Know—Know Your Numbers!

Did you know?

It is important to know your name, address, and phone number, so you'll be prepared in an emergency.

You will need

Your address, area code, and phone number
I Know Chant, page 121, copied onto white paper

What do you think?

If I practice chanting the I Know Chant, I (will) or (won't) be able to remember my address and phone number.

Now you are ready to

1. Ask an adult to write your address and phone number on the I Know Chant paper.
2. Practice saying the first line with your address until you can remember it.
3. Practice the second line with your city and state until you can remember them.
4. Say the first two lines together. Now you know your whole address!
5. Practice saying the third line with your area code until you can remember it.
6. Practice saying the fourth line with your phone number until you can remember it.
7. Say the four lines together. Now you know the whole chant. Practice it as much as you can, so you will always remember this important information.

Brain exercise

When I learned the whole chant, I felt . . .

I Know Chant

My name, address, and phone number

_____ is my home,
(address)

_____ is where I roam.
(city and state)

_____ is my area code,
(area code)

and it's _____ to call my abode.
(phone number)

Healthy Me, © 1999. Published by Chicago Review Press, Inc., 800-888-7471.

Activity Goal	Health Note	Key to Success	Hint
To teach children their addresses and phone numbers.	This information could be vital to a child's safety.	Children need to practice the chant as often as possible. Adults need to positively reinforce practicing whenever possible.	Make the chant a fun activity by using drumbeats or hand claps at the end of each line.

② Telephone Booth—A Field Trip

Did you know?
If you need to reach your parents or another adult, you can always dial 0 from a telephone booth. The operator will help you place a collect call to the adult or reach the police if it is an emergency.

You will need
Telephone booth
An adult

What do you think?
If I go up to a telephone booth and dial 0, the operator (will) or (won't) be able to help me.

Now you are ready to
1. Go with an adult to the nearest telephone booth. Can you reach up and pick up the phone? Can you see the 0?
2. Dial 0 and tell the operator you are doing a drill with an adult in case you ever get lost. Ask the operator what you should do if you were in a situation where you didn't have any money and you needed to talk to your parents or another adult.
3. Ask the adult to talk with the operator to let him or her know everything is OK.
4. Hang up the phone and see if your fingers can reach the 9-1-1. If not, don't worry—you can always dial 0 and the operator will connect you to 911 in an emergency.

Brain exercise
When I talked with the operator, I felt . . .

Activity Goal

To practice dialing from a telephone booth.

Health Note

If a child is lost, he or she can dial 911 from the phone booth. The police will come and help the child. If the child cannot reach the 9-1-1, dialing 0 will get the same results. The 0 is much easier to reach.

Key to Success

Children need to be able to reach the phone and the 0 button. In order to reach the 0 in the telephone booths tested, children had to be able to extend a finger to the height of 3 feet, 10 inches.

Hint

Children feel much more comfortable about phone booths after this field trip. Operators were happy to answer any questions.

3 Dial 911

Did you know?

Dialing 911 could save your life or the life of another person.

You will need

Practice telephone (not hooked to telephone line)

What do you think?

If I practice dialing 911, it (will) or (won't) be easier for me to dial in a real emergency.

Now you are ready to

1. Think about a situation where you might need to dial 911. Talk to an adult about these situations.

2. Take the practice telephone (make sure it isn't plugged into the wall) and practice dialing 911. Where are the numbers? Is it easy to dial 911? Try it until it feels natural to your fingers to dial that number.

3. If you need to call for help, now you'll know how to dial the right number.

Brain exercise

When I dialed 911, my fingers . . .

Activity Goal	Health Note	Key to Success	Hint
To give children the opportunity to do a practice drill dialing 911.	Knowing how to dial 911 can save a life.	This activity needs to be supervised by an adult. There needs to be discussion about the proper and improper use of 911.	It is important to keep a 911 sticker on or near the telephone. Placing red dot stickers on the telephone buttons for 911 works well also.

Make an Emergency Magnet

You will need
911 card, page 126, copied onto bright yellow card stock
Scissors
Bright markers
Laminating equipment (optional)
Self-adhesive magnet

Now you are ready to
1. Cut out the 911 card.
2. Use markers to decorate the 911 in big bright colors.
3. Decorate the card with markers. Make sure that the 911 shows up well.
4. If you can, laminate the card. Place a self-adhesive magnet on the back of the card.
5. Place the card in a special spot on your refrigerator.

Activity Goal
To place the emergency number 911 in a spot where the child and other family members will see it every day.

Health Note
The more often children are exposed to the 911 number, the more likely it will be second nature for them to use it in an emergency.

Key to Success
Place a card in a prominent position on the refrigerator.

Hint
Ask children to teach younger siblings about the importance of 911 and when it is appropriate to use it.

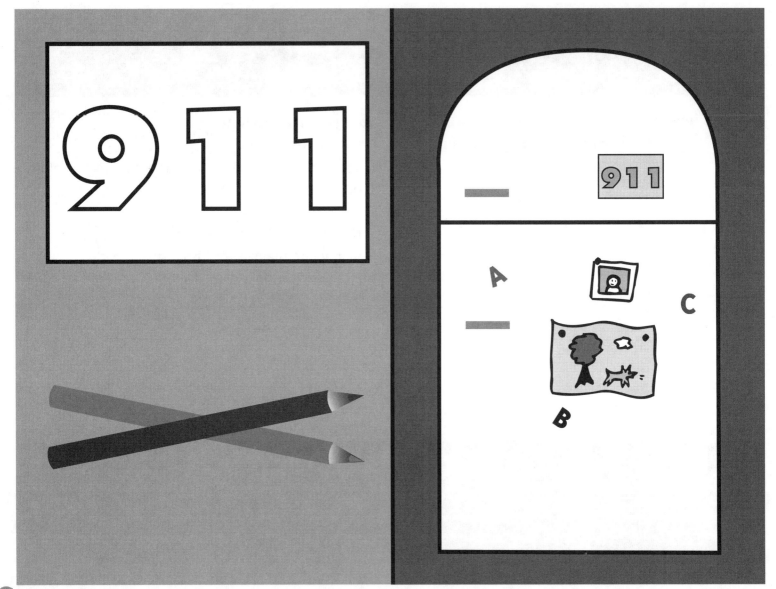

5 Check It Out—Find the Exits

Did you know?
It is important to find the exits in any building you enter. If there is an emergency, you will know how to get out of the building.

You will need
Exit Board, page 128, copied onto card stock
Pencil

What do you think?
If I go into a building, I (will) or (won't) be able to find the exits.

Now you are ready to
1. Think about why it might be important to know where the exits for a building are located. Talk to an adult about the importance of exits.
2. Go into the grocery store with an adult. Look for the big EXIT signs in the building. Remember where the exits are located in this building.
3. Make a check mark on your Exit Board for this type of building.
4. In the next building you enter, find the exits with an adult. Make a check mark on your Exit Board.
5. Look for exits everywhere you go.

Brain exercise
When I looked for the exits in different buildings, I . . .

Activity Goal	Health Note	Key to Success	Hint
To make a habit of locating exits whenever the child is in a building.	Identifying exits can save your life in a fire or other disaster.	Initially, adults will need to help children to locate the exits.	If the adult makes this a priority, so will the child.

My Exit Board

Check It Out — Find the Exits

School

House

Church

Movie Theater

Hospital

Shopping Mall

Hotel

Restaurant

Grocery Store

Library

Bus

Airplane

Healthy Me, © 1999. Published by Chicago Review Press, Inc., 800-888-7471.

6 Safety Belts—Buckle Up

Did you know?
Safety belts save many lives every year.

You will need
2 small toy pickup trucks
2 small toy figures, like Lego people
Masking tape

What do you think?
If the two trucks collide, the strapped-in toy person (will) or (won't) fly out of the truck.

Now you are ready to
1. Place a toy person in the truck bed. Strap it in with masking tape.
2. Place the other toy person in the bed of the other truck without strapping it in.
3. Make the trucks collide. What happened? Did the strapped-in toy figure get hurt? What happened to the toy figure that wasn't strapped in?

Brain exercise
When the toy figure that wasn't strapped into the truck hit the other truck, it . . .

Activity Goal	Health Note	Key to Success	Hint
To graphically show the consequences of not wearing a safety belt.	Your safety belt needs to be placed below your waist so that it won't harm your internal organs if you are in a car accident.	One of the toy figures needs to be securely strapped to the truck.	Allow children to experiment by themselves. Small Lego toy figures work very well in this activity.

7 Handy Helmet—Happy Head

Did you know?
Bicycle helmets save kids' lives every day.

You will need
1 plastic container of Silly Putty
1 heavy, large book

What do you think?
If I drop the book on a ball of Silly Putty in its plastic container, the Silly Putty (will) or (won't) be smashed.

Now you are ready to
1. Take the Silly Putty out of its container. Roll it into a ball shape. Place it on a flat, uncarpeted floor. Pick up the book and carefully drop it straight down onto the Silly Putty. What happened?
2. Roll the Silly Putty back into a ball shape. Place it inside its plastic container. Put it on the floor. Pick up the book and carefully drop it straight down onto the Silly Putty.
3. Open up the container. Was the ball hurt? Was the plastic container hurt?
4. What was the difference between the unprotected Silly Putty and the protected Silly Putty? How does this remind you of a bicycle helmet?

Brain exercise
The Silly Putty in the plastic container . . .

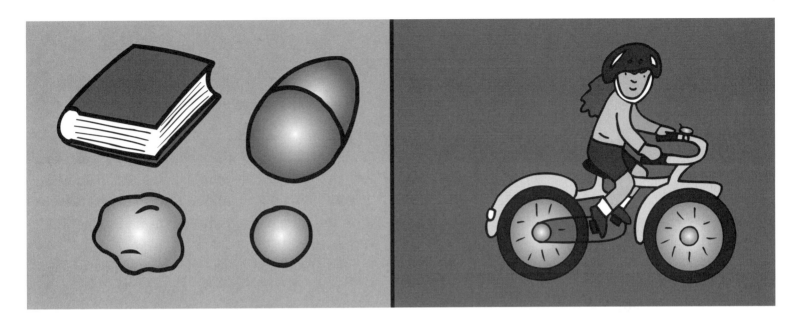

Activity Goal

To show the importance of wearing a bicycle helmet for protection.

Health Note

Helmets should fit snugly and be placed low on the forehead.

Key to Success

Use a heavy book to demonstrate the impact of two objects hitting each other.

Hint

There are many ways to demonstrate this concept. One variation uses boiled eggs, one in a sandwich bag, the other under a plastic bowl. In another variation, an unprotected cantaloupe and a cantaloupe buckled into a bicycle helmet are dropped from a height of six feet or so onto a hard floor.

8 Perfect Fit—Try It On!

Did you know?
Wearing a helmet when bicycling can help prevent injuries to your head in a fall or crash.

You will need
Your bicycle helmet

What do you think?
If I wear my helmet properly, I (will) or (won't) be better protected than if I don't wear it properly.

Now you are ready to
1. Put the helmet on so that it sits evenly between your ears and rests low on your forehead. It should be only about 2 finger-widths above your eyebrow.
2. Place the foam pads inside your helmet so that is very snug and comfortable.
3. Tighten and adjust the chin strap as snugly as you can, using the front and back straps. The straps should be positioned right under the ears.

Brain exercise
When I wore my helmet properly, my helmet felt . . .

Activity Goal	Health Note	Key to Success	Hint
To provide the helmet fitting instructions suggested by helmet manufacturers.	Helmets should be worn when using bikes, skates, roller blades, skis, and in a number of other sports.	Make sure the helmet is comfortable.	Children are more likely to wear helmets if their parents and their friends wear helmets also.

9 Safety Signs

Did you know?
Symbols and signs tell us very important information without using words.

You will need
Safety Symbols and Signs board, page 134, copied onto white card stock

Partner

What do you think?
If I look at the Safety Symbols and Signs Board, I (will) or (won't) know what the symbols mean.

Now you are ready to
1. Look at the symbols on the Safety Symbols and Signs board.
2. Choose one symbol and tell your partner what you think it means.
3. Go through as many signs as you can.
4. Talk to an adult about the signs. Were you right about their meanings?

Brain exercise
When I looked at the signs, I . . .

Activity Goal	Health Note	Key to Success	Hint
To identify important safety signs.	Most safety signs require no reading skill.	Children need to discuss these signs with an adult and then try to locate the signs in their own neighborhoods.	Use this as an outing Bingo Board. Children really enjoy looking for signs. Add new signs to a Bingo Board you design.

Safety Symbols and Signs

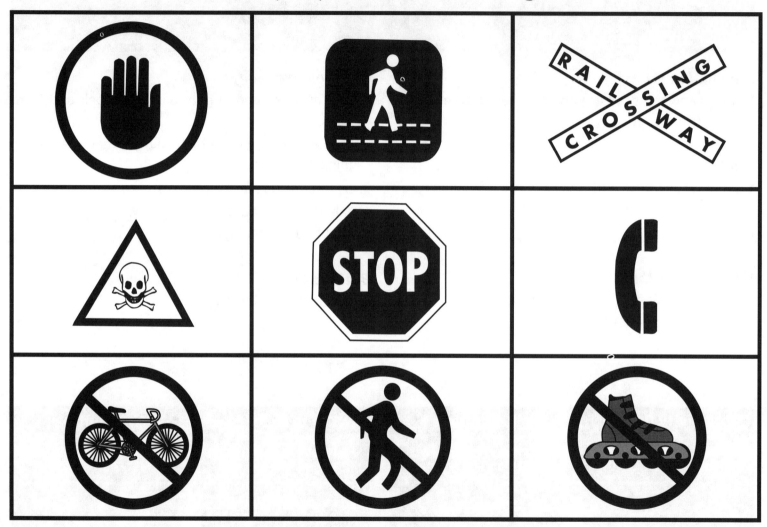

10 Look Both Ways

Did you know?
It is very important to look both ways before you cross a street.

You will need
Look Both Ways Song, page 136
Partner (one needs to be able to read)

What do you think?
If I look both ways before I cross a street, I (will) or (won't) see cars coming.

Now you are ready to
1. Read the song's words with your partner.
2. Think about the words.
3. Do you think it is important to play it safe? Do you always look both ways?
4. Sing the song with your partner.
5. Think about the words when you are getting ready to cross the street.

Brain exercise
When I cross the street, I . . .

Activity Goal	Health Note	Key to Success	Hint
To reinforce good safety habits.	It is very important that children are aware of cars as they cross the street. In some countries, children are required to wear bright yellow and carry tall signs as they cross the street.	Children need to discuss crossing safety with an adult.	Use this as a fun song to sing when you go on an outing.

Look Both Ways Song

Look both ways! Look both ways!
Before you walk, before you walk!
Cars might not see you!
Cars might not see you!
So play it safe, play it safe!

Sung to "Are You Sleeping?"

11 Buddy Up!—My Poster

You will need
A large sheet of construction paper
Markers or crayons

Now you are ready to
1. Write your name on the back of the paper. Write "Buddy Up!" at the top of your construction paper.
2. Think about why it is important to always be with a buddy when you walk or play outside.
3. Talk to a friend and an adult about this.
4. Draw pictures of doing things with your friends.
5. Save your poster and display it somewhere important to you.

Activity Goals	Health Note	Key to Success	Hint
To think about the importance of the "buddy system." To identify buddies.	It is important for a child's safety to buddy up rather than venturing out alone.	Discuss the "buddy system" with children before they make the poster.	Use safety examples from nature. Many animals travel together for protection.

You will need

Emergency Numbers sheet, copied onto card stock (laminate when finished, if possible)

Picture of you

Ink pad

Soap

Water

Towel

Photocopier

Now you are ready to

1. Write your name in on the top line of your Emergency Numbers card.

2. Ask an adult to help you with filling in all of the other information.

3. Find a recent picture and glue it onto the card.

4. Ask an adult to help you make your thumbprint and fingerprints. Wash your hands with soap and water to get the ink off them.

5. Copy the card so you can have an extra copy at home. Laminate the cards if possible to help protect them.

6. Now you have your own Emergency Numbers cards. Put one in your backpack pocket and leave one at home where it is easy to see.

Activity Goal	Health Note	Key to Success	Hint
To make a list of emergency information.	Children need to know how to get in touch with parents or relatives if there is a problem.	Keep this emergency number sheet posted on the refrigerator as well as in the backpack.	Make this a fun activity for the children. Adults can make their own cards.

My Emergency Numbers Card

Emergency Numbers

Emergency = 911   My Home (___)_____

Mother's Name _____   (___)_____

Father's Name _____   (___)_____

Relative's Name _____   (___)_____

Friend's Name _____   (___)_____

Doctor's Name _____   (___)_____

Insurance Identification _____

My Picture

My Fingerprints

Thumb	Pointer	Middle	Ring	Baby

Healthy Me, © 1999. Published by Chicago Review Press, Inc., 800-888-7471.

You will need

My Safety Certificate, page 141, copied onto card stock
Pencil or pen

Now you are ready to

1. Go through every statement on the certificate with an adult.

2. When you can say that each statement on the certificate is true for you, you will qualify for the safety certificate.

3. Ask an adult to sign the certificate and put it up on your wall.

Activity Goal	Health Note	Key to Success	Hint
To positively reinforce good safety behavior.	If children have practiced these 10 items, they will be better prepared for many emergencies than most children and adults.	Work with the children to accomplish each activity.	Make the certificate a big deal. Do something special to celebrate this event.

My Safety Certificate

_____ is a Safe and Sound Kid!

____ I practiced dialing 911 for an emergency.

____ I know my address and phone number.

____ I have practiced dialing 0 at a phone booth.

____ I look both ways when I cross the street.

____ I know where building exits are located.

____ I always wear my safety belt.

____ I always wear my helmet when I ride my bike.

____ I carry my backpack information card.

____ I always use the "buddy system."

____ I never talk to strangers.

Certified on _____

By _____

Safe and Sound Kid!

Healthy Me, © 1999. Published by Chicago Review Press, Inc., 800-888-7471.

Read All About It

Clean Machine

Author	Title	Publisher
Judi Barrett	*Pickles to Pittsburgh*	Atheneum Books, 1997
Melvin Berger	*Germs Make Me Sick*	Crowell, 1985
Vicki Cobb	*Keeping Clean*	Lippincott, 1989
Eric Houghton	*The Backwards Watch*	Orchard Books, 1992
Bobi Katz	*Germs! Germs! Germs!*	Scholastic, 1996
Mercer Mayer	*Bubble, Bubble*	Four Winds Press, 1980
Diane Patterson	*Soap and Suds*	Knopf, 1984
Patty Wolcott	*The Marvelous Mud Washing Machine*	Addison-Wesley, 1974
Elvira Woodruff	*Show & Tell*	Holiday House, 1991

Healthy Chompers

Author	Title	Publisher
Marc Brown	*Arthur's Tooth*	Monthly Press, 1985
Jo Carson	*Pulling My Leg*	Orchard Books, 1990
Roger Duvoisin	*Crocus*	Knopf, 1977
Paul Showers	*How Many Teeth?*	Crowell, 1962
Audrey Wood	*Tooth Fairy*	Greenwillow Books, 1977

Nutritious and Delicious

Author	Title	Publisher
Judi Barrett	*Pickles to Pittsburgh*	Atheneum Books, 1997
Sandra Belton	*May'naise Sandwiches & Sunshine Tea*	Four Winds Press, 1994
Carol Ryrie Brink	*Goody O'Grumpity*	North-South, 1994
Cheryl Chapman	*Pass the Fritters, Critters*	Four Winds Press, 1993
Tomie dePaola	*The Popcorn Book*	Holiday, 1993
Lois Ehlert	*Eating the Alphabet*	Harcourt, 1989
Douglas Florian	*A Chef*	Greenwillow, 1991
Meredith Hooper	*A Cow, a Bee, a Cookie and Me*	Kingfisher, 1997
Loreen Leedy	*The Edible Pyramid*	Holiday, 1991
Elaine Moore	*Grandma's Garden*	Lothrop, Lee & Shepard, 1994
Marjorie Priceman	*How to Make an Apple Pie and See the World*	Knopf, 1994
Gina Rodriguez	*Green Corn Tamales*	Hispanic Books, 1994
Maureen Roffey	*Mealtime*	Four Winds Press, 1989
Cynthia Rylant	*Mr. Putter and Tabby Bake the Cake*	Harcourt, 1994
Anne Shelby	*Potluck*	Orchard Books, 1991
Peggy Thomson	*Siggy's Spaghetti Works*	Tambourine, 1993

Product Information

Clean Machine
Glo Germ
Glo Germ Company
PO Box 537
Moab, UT 84532
1-800-842-6622
http:/www.glogerm.com
Lit #1002 $49.00 (prices coming down
soon for smaller kit)

Healthy Chompers
Disclosing tablets
Butler Red-Cote
John O. Butler Company
4635 W. Foster Avenue
Chicago, IL 60630
$2.92 for 10

General
Handheld 30X microscope
Cuisenaire/Dale Seymour
1-800-237-0338
NC088021 (Tasco) $9.50

Acknowledgments

Thanks to:

Debbie Braaten, physical education specialist, Christa McAuliffe Elementary School, Redmond, Washington, for her consultation and support.

Jonathan Levey, D.D.S., Family Dentistry, Issaquah, Washington, for professional consultation and donation of the dental supplies needed to test chomper activities.

William M. Muse, biologist, for his text consultation.

Linda Matthews for her wonderful editing.

Maureen O'Brien for her helpful comments.

Gid Palmer for his flexibility and support.

Margaret Piela, RN, for her wonderful nutrition ideas.

Joyce Roeder, RN, school health specialist, Lake Washington School District, Redmond, Washington for consultation on the nutrition chapter.

Evelyn Sansky for her constant love and support.

The staff at the Inn at Semi-ah-moo for their support during text revision.

Stephen Yoo and Nick Palmer for their backseat editing ideas in the carpool.

Thanks to the following for their flexibility and suggestions, and for opening up their classrooms to countless hours of activity testing. This book could not have been written without their support and the contributions of their eager students.

Mrs. Blakley, a first-grade teacher at Christa McAuliffe Elementary School, Redmond, Washington.

Mrs. Brown, a kindergarten teacher at Elizabeth Blackwell Elementary School, Redmond, Washington.

Mrs. Sylvestal, a second-grade teacher at Samantha Smith Elementary School, Redmond, Washington.

Thanks to Mrs. Hanson, a seventh-grade teacher at Redmond Junior High School in Redmond, Washington, for allowing me the opportunity to go through the writing process with her brilliant students as content editors. Her students helped with the reviewing, testing, and problem-solving issues in the text. Their practical suggestions and problem-solving efforts contributed significantly to the writing of *Healthy Me*.

Student Contributors

Mrs. Brown's kindergarten class
John Castle
Anthony Delie
Kara Edwards
Nikolas Grasst
Alexis Guches
Patrick Leake
John Lee
Matthew Loh
Dylan Lovell
Chelsy Martin
Nathaniel McCammant
David Parkinson
Jeremy Rodney
Katelin Rolls
Leda Salaimani
Jacob Salley
Matthew Shore
Lacy Sigman
Erin Smith
Robert Spaulding
Clarissa Stevens
Nicola Vann

Mrs. Blakley's first-grade class
Kelsea Asher
Blake Baylor
Zachary Byrski
Michael Cofano
Garrett Daily
Alexandra Dorsey
Michelle Jackson
Evan Lee
Ian McClung
Riley Peronto
Keisha Peterson
Daniel Preston
Isabell Sakamoto
Cori Shull
Rio Simone
Emily Skubitz
Shayne Smith
Andrew Steyer
Ethan Thomas
Emily Vivian

Mrs. Sylvestal's second-grade class
Tyler Andrews
Will Baker
Raphael Bamickel
Megan Beebe
Julia Bicknell
Corbin Brokaw
Keenan Clinch
Matthew Fuget
Christopher Gordon
Chad Gray
Madeline Harig
Erik Hawes
Laura Hedeen
Stephanie Kyser
Tony Locascio
Alexa Marrs
Michael McDonald
Leona Mullen
Tyler Munno
Kallen Nelson
Magnus Olofsson
Elizabeth Orr
Duncan Sinclair
Chauncey Trask
Brent Tsujii
Alyssa Vaughan
Megan Winkel

Mrs. Hanson's seventh-grade student editors
Jesse Albert
Katie Buck
Clara Cantor
Dan Cantor
Jennifer Cushing
Joscelyn Doleac
Brock Erwin
Anna Eschenburg
Tammy Guo
Jesse Heilman
Andrew Hopps
Jillian Houck
Emily Hu
David Lee
Emmett Nicholas
Rob Ohlstrom
Stephanie Orrico
Tyler Sargent
Peter Simonson
Debbie Weiser
Jammie Wu

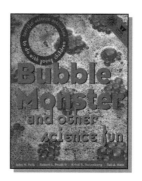

Sense-Abilities
Fun Ways to Explore the Senses
Michelle O'Brien-Palmer

Dozens of fun and original science activities that explore taste, touch, sight, smell, and hearing.

"These great ideas should be welcomed by teachers."
—*School Library Journal*

ages 4–8
ISBN 1-55652-327-0
176 pages, paper, $12.95

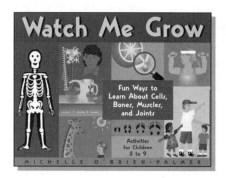

Watch Me Grow
Fun Ways to Learn About Cells, Bones, Muscles, and Joints
Michelle O'Brien-Palmer

Offering 60 activities to explore the bones, muscles, joints, and other connective tissues, this book examines the amazing cells that make up the human body. A "growth portfolio" allows young scientists to track their growth, and silly songs and lively illustrations help them remember new words and concepts.

ages 5–9
ISBN 1-55652-367-X
152 pages, paper, $12.95